A FULNESS OF JOY

OTHER BOOKS AND BOOKS ON CASSETTE
BY RICHARD D. DRAPER:

The Savior's Prophecies

TALKS ON CASSETTE

The Book of Revelation: Testifying of Christ

Keys to Understanding the Book of Revelation

A FULNESS OF JOY

RICHARD D. DRAPER

Covenant Communications, Inc.

Cover tapestry & pattern, *Woodpecker pattern (for an Arras tapestry)* by William Morris, *William Morris Full-Color Patterns and Designs,* Dover Publications.

Cover design copyrighted 2002 by Covenant Communications, Inc.

Published by Covenant Communications, Inc.
American Fork, Utah

Printed in Canada
First Printing: February 2002

09 08 07 06 05 04 03 02   10 9 8 7 6 5 4 3 2 1

ISBN 1-57734-994-6

Library of Congress Cataloging-in-Publication Data

Dedicated to my mother,
Florence Shepherd Draper
who personifies the virtues of love and joy.

CONTENTS

Preface...1

Chapter 1: *Happiness, Joy, and Exaltation*.................................5

Chapter 2: *The Inward Fountain of Joy*...................................21

Chapter 3: *Joy and the Atonement*..35

Chapter 4: *Love and Joy*...53

Chapter 5: *The Pure Love of Christ*.......................................63

Chapter 6: *Love and Calling and Election*...............................81

Chapter 7: *The Commandment to Love*.................................109

Chapter 8: *Overcoming the Impediments to Love and Joy*.........133

Chapter Notes..143

Index 179

PREFACE

My wife is responsible for this book, at least indirectly. Oh, she did not say, "You seem to have way too much time on your hands. Why don't you go write a book?" Rather, it was something she said to one of my children that grabbed my mind and would not let go. Neither of us knew at the time that a book would grow out of her comment; we were just living life with our children and doing our best to raise them in "the way of the Lord." Our son, Matthew, then in his seventeenth year, delighted in pestering his mother with feigned teenage angst about life and its ultimate meaning. He seemed sure this was a way to needle her because no one could know the answer; it was too big and wonderful for anyone to know. She always shrugged off his teasing with good-natured humor. But on this day he once again teased her, asking, "What is the purpose of it all?" She responded on a very serious note.

I was in another room at the moment, but could clearly hear the conversation. Here he was asking the age old question, "What is the meaning of life?" My overactive imagination could picture my son toiling up a mountain in search of the great guru who could divine universal secrets and answer the unanswerable questions. What I did not realize until that moment was that the great guru did not live on a mountain top—she lived in my house. Indeed, I had married her.

With some force (perhaps growing out of his relentless teasing), my wife informed my son that if he did not know the answer to that question, he had not been listening closely enough to his parents. I appreciated the fact that she included me as one of those who knew the answer to the question of life's meaning, but I have to confess, I didn't think I knew it. The question was too big, too all encompassing, too complex for me to know the answer. She, however, knew it. "The whole meaning of life," she told him emphatically, "can be summarized in two small words, and the sooner you understand these, the easier your life will be. Those two words are 'love' and 'joy.' Your job," she went on, "is to choose the path that leads to both." I wasn't sure if her answer satisfied him, but it struck me with force as something quite profound and worth exploring further.

I teased her a little later about being the great guru who could summarize the purpose of life in just two words. Under my playful nudging, she explained her feelings and insights more fully. She said that, as she saw it, joy was the objective for all existence—not just for humankind, but for all living things. I remembered that John the Revelator had seen in heaven, "the happiness of man, and of beasts, and of creeping things, and of the fowls of the air" (D&C 77:2). She went on to explain that the way God brings us to joy is through love: His and the Savior's love for us, and our love for them, ourselves, and each other. Her words cemented fragments of thoughts and pieces of questions into clarifications and answers in my mind. These, in turn, led to other questions. With her insight and help, I began the investigation that resulted in this book.

While this book is *not* a "how to" book on happiness, marital relations, or success in romance (though I hope it will contribute to these areas), it *is* a study of two gospel principles—dare I say the two most important gospel principles—that are seldom investigated in their doctrinal context. This book investigates the relationship of love and joy in bringing about God's purposes as far as humankind is concerned.

I appreciate those who became part of the team that helped produce this work. My thanks go out to my research assistants Leann Boone, Heather Vivian, and Rachael Carver, who looked up sources, checked footnotes, and otherwise did technical and editing work; to my daughter, Jessica, and my secretary, Rachael Porter, who took a rough manuscript and turned it into a work I was not ashamed to show others; to my colleagues in Religious Education at Brigham Young University, S. Kent Brown, Larry E. Dahl, Paul Y. Hoskisson, Kent P. Jackson, Gaye Strathearn, and Dennis Wright, who read parts of this manuscript and offered helpful suggestions and criticisms; and to my wife Barbara, that great guru, whose insights sparked the whole effort. Finally, I give special thanks to my mother, Florence Draper, and Aunt Josephine Tidwell, for reading the whole manuscript to make sure it communicated.

I have made every attempt to be in harmony with the teachings of The Church of Jesus Christ of Latter-day Saints and to keep the ideas presented in this book doctrinally sound. However, I alone am responsible for the conclusions drawn in this work.

CHAPTER 1

HAPPINESS, JOY, *and* EXALTATION

THE REASON ADAM FELL

What is the purpose of life? People of many cultures and times have asked that question, yet today the general feeling is that there is no answer, only speculation. Some see the question as absurd, even laughable, while others take it more seriously. A few feel they have found the answer and are willing, even eager, to enlighten those who ask. Among these are rock stars, politicians, and even gambling lords. So, too, is the Savior through His prophets. This book explores the Lord's answer, one so plain and simple that it is often overlooked or discounted, yet, when understood, fully satisfies the question. We find His answer in the Book of Mormon and after we have reviewed it, we will explore its significance.

Lehi made a seemingly simple statement when he declared: "Adam fell that men might be; and men are, that they might have joy" (2 Ne. 2:25). The prophet's thought is so succinct that it is easy to dismiss or pass over it without realizing its full significance. Here in just fourteen words, Lehi answers the age old question, what is the purpose of life? In order to appreciate the pertinence of his thought, allow me to expand on it. Adam made a conscious and deliberate decision to fall. His objective was to bring humankind into being. If Adam had not made that choice, there would have been no humans on this planet—ever.

By humans, I mean "mortals." The word stem comes from the Latin *mors,* meaning "death." Lehi did not use the word "mortals." He used the word "men," but given the context in which he used the word, he had mortals in mind—people who would occupy this world for a brief time and then die.

But was death to be the end of existence? If so, why bother bringing humans into being at all? The answer is that only the physical part of "men" is mortal, and even that is restored at resurrection. Lehi looked beyond mortality to find meaning and purpose in existence as a whole. In so doing, he taught us that we are moving toward a grand objective. God has a greater purpose for His children than their experiencing the mere flash of mortality. Lehi taught us that the object of existence, both in mortality and beyond, is to gain joy. In that one little word, Lehi summed up the purpose of life.

Joseph Smith, the translator of Lehi's words, paraphrased the prophet's thought this way: "Happiness is the object and design of our existence; and will be the end thereof, if we pursue the path that leads to it."[1] The Lord seems very interested in whether or not we are happy; thus He has laid down a great plan to bring us to that state.

So what do we mean by "happiness"? Happiness, along with the related words blessedness, felicity, beatitude and bliss, denotes the pleasurable satisfaction which arises from a state of well-being. "Happiness" is a more generic term and, while it can apply to almost any state of pleasurable enjoyment or well-being, it more particularly describes the feeling arising from security, accomplishment, or obtaining a wish or goal.[2] For those whose wish or desire is eternal life, God becomes a ready partner who clearly defines the way.

Happiness, however, was not the word Lehi used. Under inspiration, he said that "men are, that they might have joy." There is a difference between happiness and joy.[3] As we noted above, Joseph Smith paraphrased Lehi's statement by using the word "happiness."[4] In the Prophet's context, joy and happiness are synonyms, and we should understand that they have similar meanings. Even so, there are differences in nuance which deserve exploration and show that joy more accurately expresses Lehi's intent. Let us see why.

Happiness describes the feeling associated with a state of well-being.[5] When that state is unachieved, threatened, or disrupted, we are not happy. Joy is the agreeable emotion which accompanies the possession, acquisition, or expectation of something good or very desirable.[6] Joy can, but does not necessarily, arise out of present circumstances. We can also feel joy over something we anticipate. Consider the well-known question God asked Job:

> Where wast thou when I laid the foundations of the
> earth? declare, if thou hast understanding. Who hath laid
> the measures thereof, if thou knowest? or who hath
> stretched the line upon it? Whereupon are the foundations
> thereof fastened? or who laid the corner stone thereof;
> When the morning stars sang together, and all the sons of
> God shouted for joy? (Job 38:4–7).

In this case, it was not just the creation that brought joy to the children of God, but its anticipation.

Happiness relies heavily on the present; joy much less so. Joy adds the dimensions of acquisition and continuance to happiness. "Those who have died in Jesus Christ," Joseph Smith taught, "may expect to enter into all that fruition of joy when they come forth, which they possessed or anticipated here."[7] Thus, the future will bequeath a fulness of the joy that was either won or anticipated in the present. The Savior himself endured all things, including the cross, "for the joy that was set before him" (Heb. 12:2). What we must understand is that sometimes we have to forsake happiness for the moment so we can experience lasting joy in the future.

Joy is closely akin to pleasure and delight, when these words are taken in a positive sense.[8] Pleasure denotes a feeling of gratification or satisfaction, but does not necessarily imply continued gladness or happiness. It is a transitory state, whereas both joy and happiness are more permanent. That is not to say that joy, happiness, and pleasure cannot exist simultaneously. Often the excitement of the senses or the mind contributes to positive happiness;[9] however, because pleasure is usually fleeting, it is generally not *accurately* associated with joy and happiness. Giving in to sensual pleasure outside the Lord's bounds may bring temporary enjoyment, but it also causes long-lasting pain. As Alma told Corianton, "wickedness never was happiness" (Alma 41:10). Wickedness can never lead us to a state of permanent well-being, so neither happiness nor joy can ever grow out of it.

The word "delight" suggests a stronger sense of liveliness and intensity of feeling than pleasure. However, delight is an emotional state which is even less stable and enduring. Joy adds constancy to both pleasure and delight, making them enduring. Thus it is only in the presence of joy that delight or pleasure can be positive, for joy alone transcends that which is fleeting or worldly. Although many people use the word "joy" in place of pleasure and still more often in place of delight, it is more appropriate to use joy "when a deep-rooted, rapturous emotion is implied or when the happiness is so great as to be almost painful in its intensity."[10] We should never divorce joy from pleasure or happiness, but neither should we think that joy is dependent upon them. Joy can thrive outside a state of well-being because it is the extreme feeling which comes from the fulfillment of all for which one has striven and been expectant.[11]

A COMMON MISUNDERSTANDING

There is a mistaken notion that floats around the Church from time to time. It is based on wishful thinking and a misunderstanding of the scriptures. Yet it sounds sweet—the way we would like life to be. I was impressed with how deceptively well it was taught one day in a seminary devotional. I was an area supervisor for the seminary system in Arizona at the time, and one of my tasks was to visit the seminaries in my area, working with students and teachers.

A young man, good-looking, sincere, and innocent, had the thought that day. He spoke of the importance of being an example to those in the high school. He then promised his fellow students that if they would live the gospel, the Savior would shield them from all harm and trials, miracles would follow them, and they would never know sorrow or pain. He then closed with a tender story of how his father, being forewarned by the Spirit, had been able to save his daughter from a fall that might have resulted in her death.

After class, the teacher, bubbling with enthusiasm, told me that he planned on using part of his class period the next day to amplify the student's thought. He would drive home the wonderful testimony that gospel living protected one from the vicissitudes of life. He went on to tell me of a wonderful moment when a relative of his was healed through miraculous means. He said he would build his lesson around that story.

I felt very uncomfortable with what he intended to teach. I asked him if anyone in his family had ever experienced trials, hardships, disappointments, or failures. Well, yes, they had, he admitted. Was it because they were a pack of sinners? I asked. Well, no, he conceded, but he was sure that if they had been totally righteous, none would have suffered. I asked him to look at the witness of the scriptures, our Church history and his own life concerning this idea. I told him that we are here to find our way to a fulness of joy. Such joy often comes from anticipating a future reward that grows out of the necessary trials of the present. I went on to explain the following.

JOY IN THIS LIFE OFTEN GROWS THROUGH TRIALS

We must not allow the idea that joy arises partly out of anticipation to overshadow the fact that we can and should try to achieve a state of joy in the present. Adam knew that it was possible. Under the power of the Holy Spirit, he prophesied, "Blessed be the name of God, for because of my transgression my eyes are opened, and in this life I shall have joy, and again in the flesh I shall see God" (Moses 5:10). Eve's response confirmed her husband's view: "Were it not for our transgression we never should have had seed, and never should have known good and evil, and the joy of our redemption, and the eternal life which God giveth unto all the obedient" (Moses 5:11). Adam looked to the immediate future ("in this life I shall have joy"), while Eve looked beyond to the "joy of our redemption" and resurrection.

Interestingly, Adam and Eve had to fall to find joy. The paradise of Eden, which so many view in false idyllic terms, was in reality a joyless place. I do believe they were happy in the sense that, until Satan caused certain dissonance, they felt a secure sense of well-being. However, though the garden provided Adam and Eve with every necessity, though they walked with God, though they knew neither threat nor fear, though they knew no sorrow, still they knew no joy. As Lehi explained, had they not fallen, "they would have remained in a state of innocence, having no joy, for they knew no misery; doing no good, for they knew no sin" (2 Ne. 2:23). Note that the unproductive innocence of the garden proved an infertile soil in which the plant of joy could never fully flower.[12]

The joy Lehi had in mind, according to B. H. Roberts, had "to arise out of man's rough and thorough knowledge of evil, of sin;

through knowing misery, sorrow, pain and suffering; through seeing good and evil locked in awful conflict; through a consciousness of having chosen in that conflict the better part, the good; and not only in having chosen it, but in having wedded it by eternal compact; made it his by right of conquest over evil."[13]

In this way, Adam's fall placed humankind in a position to gain joy in this life. Our Church authorities have stressed that the acquisition of joy often arises out of the vicissitudes and weakness of mortality. Again, Elder Roberts confirmed that:

> [M]en learn to appreciate the joys of prosperity by drinking of the cup of adversity; they learn to prize the boon of health, by languishing upon the bed of affliction; they learn the value of wealth, by experiencing want and poverty; the sweets of life are rendered still more sweet by the draughts of bitterness men are compelled to drink; and the ever intermittent gleams of sunshine are made more bright to the renewing storms which darken the sky.[14]

In this sense, a person could go through a period of unhappiness and still possess joy, the present sorrow being no match for the jubilation which will come. This is the context in which we can best understand Peter's counsel to the Saints of his day. Encouraging them, he explained that they had achieved "an inheritance incorruptible" in heaven which would never fade. Even so, "ye are in heaviness through manifold temptations:[15] That the trial of your faith, being much more precious than of gold that perisheth, though it be tried with fire, might be found unto praise and honour and glory at the appearing of Jesus Christ: Whom having not seen, ye love; in whom, though now ye see him not, yet believing, ye rejoice with joy unspeakable" (1 Pet.1:4, 6–8).

In Peter's words we see that these early Saints had achieved the assurance of "an inheritance incorruptible" that would never "fade away" because it was "reserved in heaven" for them. Though continued faithfulness was still necessary, they had already secured one blessing: the assurance that their reward was waiting. In this they "greatly rejoiced." He did not mean that their lives were free of difficulties or challenges; however, these were to be but trials of faith which would assure "the salvation of your souls." We get the feeling that the distress under which these Saints were living did not allow for much happiness. Nonetheless, we see that they were filled, to rephrase Peter's words, with an inexpressible and glorious joy (v. 8).[16] Thus, it was not the social circumstances in which they were living, but their spiritual condition which brought them joy in the present.

JOY AND SERVICE

The key to finding the joy which endures even through unhappiness, such as that found by the early Saints, comes through Christlike service. As Elder Neal A. Maxwell has so clearly stated, "Our joy depends upon the degree to which we are like Him and serve as He did, even amid trial."[17] The scriptures advise us that glory comes only after tribulation: "For after much tribulation come the blessings. Wherefore the day cometh that ye shall be crowned with much glory; the hour is not yet, but is nigh at hand" (D&C 58:4).

There is a reason why one can have present joy while going through a period of unhappiness. Joy arises from the development of self and others. As Elder Roberts said, "It is the purpose of earth-existence to secure [joy], remembering from what it is to arise—from the highest possible development—the highest conceivable enlargement of physical, intellectual, moral and spiritual power—what other conceivable purpose for existence in earth-life could there be for eternal Intelligences than this attainment of 'joy' springing from progress?"[18]

God has declared that "this is my work and my glory—to bring to pass the immortality and eternal life of man" (Moses 1:39). In this scripture, He not only discloses the direction of His work, but also the source of His joy, which is found in allowing all to reach their full potential and to share with Him a fulness of joy.[19] Those who engage in God's work may still experience distress and even failure, but the knowledge that they are about God's work in assisting others toward an eternal goal brings joy.

In this light, we can then understand the joy of heaven. Allow me to illustrate what I mean with a personal experience. At one time in my career as a seminary teacher, I desperately wanted my students to do some soul-searching about their motives in being righteous, so I asked the question, "Why do you want to go to the celestial kingdom?" They knew many of the right answers and readily listed them off: being with the Father, the Savior, an eternal mate, and their parents (knowing how some of them were trying to break free of parents, that one made me wonder, but at least they knew the correct answer).

We analyzed their list of reasons and soon came to the conclusion that the appeal of heaven was that it promised happiness—absolute bliss. The kids just knew that they would be eternally happy if they were with God, the Savior, their parents, and especially their eternal mate, whomever that may be.

I then changed the subject and we talked of things that contributed to unhappiness. Having had some experience in the military, I dwelt for a bit on how war, destruction, and death can cause true misery. My students agreed that war does not generate happiness. I then asked if they thought there would be war in the telestial kingdom. We decided there would be no war there, that people would be secure and at peace—they would be happy. I then asked about the terrestrial kingdom. My students insisted that the inhabitants of the terrestrial kingdom would know even greater happiness than the telestial because it was a higher state of glory. Nothing would ever disturb the peace, nor, therefore, the happiness, of the terrestrial kingdom. I agreed.

Then I asked about the celestial kingdom. There was unanimity that this would be the best and happiest place of all. Nothing but peace and harmony would echo throughout the great halls of heaven. My students assured me that here all would be deliriously happy all the time. I then read them a scripture which says: "And there was war in heaven: Michael and his angels fought against the dragon; and the dragon fought and his angels, And prevailed not; neither was their place found any more in heaven. And the great dragon was cast out, that old serpent, called the Devil, and Satan, which deceiveth the whole world" (Rev. 12:7–9). We discussed this war, especially its casualties which were a "third part" of God's children. I stressed that those who died in that battle were literally the children of God. They had a God father and a God mother who cared for them deeply, but against whom they had rebelled and warred. These rebels went so far as to try to destroy all that these Gods wanted for their children.

I then asked them to imagine how God the Father must have felt. "Do you think He reveled in the destruction of His children—especially considering that the power Michael used to destroy them was the power of priesthood, God's own power?"[20] My students said He probably did not feel happy. In fact, they concluded, He probably felt tremendous sorrow and loss for those whom He loved.

I then asked my students why they wanted to go to heaven. They were no longer sure. Somehow it no longer seemed like a place where people could be assured of eternal happiness. Suddenly, it looked like a place where no one, not even Gods, were protected from sorrow, loss, or pain. Indeed, it looked like a place where people, even Gods, could find rejection, hatred, and hurt. And it is.

But this does not mean heaven is a joyless place. Joy abounds there because the Gods know that they have given full opportunity to their offspring to become all they wish to become. The point is that heaven is not a place people go to be served; it is a place they go to serve. True righteousness is selfless service. That is what I wanted my seminary students to realize. The joy of heaven grows out of serving others, and not out of whether others accept or reject that service. Therefore, the threat of the pain of hell can never hold the joy of heaven hostage.

In this we come to understand something about our omniscient God. Because He knows all things, some wonder what keeps Him from being bored to tears, but now we see how an omniscient God knowing all law and life can avoid tedium. Boredom never sets in because there is "in fact, divine delight in that 'one eternal round' which, to us, seems to be all routine and repetition. God derives His great and continuing joy and glory by increasing and advancing His creations, and not from new intellectual experiences."[21]

JOY COMES ONLY THROUGH FOLLOWING UNALTERABLE PRINCIPLES

Let me further stress the point. Joy grows out of enlarging and serving others; it can never grow out of taking from another soul.

Consider the pyromaniac. A kind of twisted pleasure momentarily grips him as he sees the power of his own destructive act, but the flash of pleasure draws its source from someone else's loss and pain. "Joy is nondeductible;" Elder Neal A. Maxwell tells us, "it is an addition to one that does not require subtraction from someone else. Unlike the pyromaniac, disciples are involved with a much different kind of Fire."[22] The fire he speaks of welds hearts and fuses souls through the flame of love. In that love and unity, a fulness of joy is found.

Elder Maxwell states further that the "conditions upon which true joy are based (joy such as He has) are fixed and cannot be altered. It is merely a question of whether or not we wish to come to terms with those conditions—now or later. It is a decision in which, in the justness of God, we are the sole determinants. When we do so decide, we are really in no position to dictate the terms of our own surrender—especially to Him who suffered for our sins, which suffering caused Him to 'bleed at every pore.'"[23]

In this light we must return again to the statement by Joseph Smith, that "happiness is the object and design of our existence; and will be the end thereof, if we pursue the path that leads to it; and this path is virtue, uprightness, faithfulness, holiness, and keeping all the commandments of God."[24] Brigham Young expressed the same idea, saying that the Saints should "strive to be righteous, not for any speculation, but because righteousness is lovely, pure, holy, beautiful, and exalting; it is designed to make the soul happy and full of joy."[25] In the end, it is when we serve for pure righteousness' sake, without thought for ourselves, that we experience a fulness of joy.

THE OPPONENT OF JOY

There is one who opposes joy and works for its obliteration. The Book of Mormon clearly exposes Satan and his desires. According to Lehi, Satan fell from heaven, in the process becoming "miserable forever;" he, therefore, "sought also the misery of all mankind" (2 Ne. 2:18). Lehi goes on to explain that men and women "are free according to the flesh; and all things are given them which are expedient unto man. And they are free to choose liberty and eternal life, through the great Mediator of all men, or to choose captivity and death, according to the captivity and power of the devil; for he seeketh that all men might be miserable like unto himself" (2 Ne. 2:27).

Misery is what Satan seeks to impose. Many feel his drive comes from a desire to win the war. Correctly, they see what we call the war in heaven as merely one battle, and insist that the war still rages. They are wrong, however, to suppose that Satan thinks he can win the war. The outcome was predetermined in that premortal battle, so winning is not what motivates him. John the Revelator knew what his motivation was; he was well acquainted with the lord of darkness and what drove him. According to John, the war in heaven ended when:

> the great dragon was cast out, that old serpent, called the Devil, and Satan, which deceiveth the whole world: he was cast out into the earth, and his angels were cast out with him. And I heard a loud voice saying in heaven, Now is come salvation, and strength, and the kingdom of our God, and the power of his Christ: for the accuser of our brethren is cast down, which accused them before our God day and night. And they overcame him by the blood of the Lamb, and by the word of their testimony; and they loved not their lives unto the death. Therefore rejoice, ye heavens, and ye that dwell in them. Woe to the inhabiters of the earth and of the sea! for the devil is come down unto you, having great wrath, because he knoweth that he hath but a short time (Rev. 12: 9–12).

There are several points in this passage of special note. The Devil is "the accuser." The word John uses here is interesting for it is the source of Lucifer's title, "Satan," which means "to put in a bad light."[26] The book of Job reveals Satan's adversarial methods as he accuses Job of righteousness based solely on expectation of reward. Note his insinuation as he says to God, "Doth Job fear God for nought? Hast not thou made an hedge about him, and about his house, and about all that he hath on every side? thou hast blessed the work of his hands, and his substance is increased in the land" (Job 1:9–10). By this means, Satan put Job's faith in a bad light. He followed this up with his challenge, "Put forth thine hand now, and touch all that he hath, and he will curse thee to thy face" (v. 11). God would not, but allowed Satan to move against the faithful man, and Satan—the adversary—certainly attacked Job, ripping from him all that was dear.

Satan desires to sift people as wheat that he might find cause to accuse them (see Luke 22:31; Alma 37:15; 3 Ne. 18:18; D&C 52:12). The idea behind the imagery is that his winnowing will reveal some sort of unwillingness on the part of the disciple to serve God, and by this means he will find reason to make his accusations. Satan will do all in his power, even trying to deceive the whole world, in order to accomplish his desires.

To combat the machinations of Satan, the Savior gives His disciples the Comforter. The word Jesus used identifies one who stands as defender and witness in behalf of the accused.[27] Often the Comforter supplies key material which gets the defendant freed. Thus, translations of "legal assistant," "advocate," "intercessor" and "one who brings comfort" all work. In a broader sense, the word designated anyone who acted as a helper, advocate, or assistant. It is in this sense that the idea of a comforter comes into play. As one calls for help,[28] the Comforter responds, thereby bringing consolation, assistance, and comfort. The task of the Comforter is to guard the disciple against, or to undo, the work of the adversary.

Another point John brings out is that the devil's wrath draws its intensity from the fact that he knows he has but a short time. All too soon, to continue the imagery of John, an angel will come, bind Satan with chains, and cast him into the abysmal pit where he will do no more evil for a millennium. (See Rev. 20:1–3). John clearly shows us that the force that drives Satan is not the hope of winning, but something much more sinister and ugly. As Lehi said, he seeks to make all men miserable. I believe Lehi's description is only partial. Misery does not quite describe the breadth of a rule based on blood and horror. A better word would be pain.

Pain is what Satan seeks to inflict. It is sweet to him; he savors its aroma. It lifts and exhilarates him, for he is sadistic through and through. This twisted pleasure has become his bread, and he flavors it with the salt of tears. The scream of the burning conscience is his butter and the agony of real and imagined wounds is his jelly. He is a billion times more itchy for pain than the Marquis de Sade (from whom the term "sadist" derives), or his modern spiritual kin who worked as butchers in Nazi death camps and Soviet gulags. When Nephi's people were brutalized with a pulverizing destruction that caused some to be buried in the sea or under mountains, or to have their bodies seared with intense flames, Christ observed, "the devil laugheth, and his angels rejoice, because of the slain" (3 Ne. 9:2). The devil is insatiable—his desire for pain is unquenchable.

It has been said, "You can't get something for nothing." To this common-sense saying Lucifer has given a diabolic twist. With him, you get nothing for something. He makes empty promises like, "Ye shall not surely die" (Moses 4:10), or, "These things shall be hidden from God."[29] Then the minute you stick your neck out—WHAM! He has your soul. But wait! Maybe you do get something in return: eternal misery.

Consider the fate of Cain, the one soul who, more than any other, allied with Satan. Seduced into believing that Satan "would do according to his commands" (Moses 5:30), Cain killed his brother. He had his moment of glory, exulting, "I am free" (Moses 5:33). But then came brutal reality, forcing him to cry, "My punishment is greater than I can bear" (Moses 5:38). Cast off from God, Cain became food for Satan's table.[30] As a fugitive and vagabond, he knew neither happiness nor joy. Such will be the fate of all who team up with the father of misery.

Allow one more tragic example to drive the point home. Korihor had it all: prestige, intelligence, wealth—wonderful gifts that Satan used to seduce Korihor and others to follow him down the same dark road. Korihor ended up a deaf and dumb beggar, suffering the full misery of ignominy. Finally, he became a highway fatality for whom hell opened wide its jaws to receive. "Thus we see," writes Mormon, "that the devil will not support his children at the last day, but doth speedily drag them down to hell" (see either Alma 30:60 or Alma 30:6–60). Misery, not joy, awaits all who follow the lord of darkness.

We would do well to heed the counsel of President Benson, who revealed that:

> [O]ne of Satan's most frequently used deceptions is the notion that the commandments of God are meant to

restrict freedom and limit happiness. Young people especially sometimes feel that the standards of the Lord are like
fences and chains, blocking them from those activities that
seem most enjoyable in life. But exactly the opposite is
true. The gospel plan is the plan by which men are brought
to a fulness of joy. This is the first concept I wish to stress:
The gospel principles are the steps and guidelines that will
help us find true happiness and joy.[31]

We must not be fooled into believing that there is some kind of
neutral ground, that there are no absolutes, that we are free to "do our
own thing." Such an attitude does not free us from Satan's grasp.
Some people really do believe that they can do it their way, but if we
watch closely, soon we will detect an emerging pattern. Those who do
their own thing follow the same road as those who do Satan's, but "in
an unconscious pattern of sobering servility."[32] They give up their
chance at joy and exaltation without even sensing the decision. "Thus
the devil cheateth their souls, and leadeth them away carefully down
to hell" (2 Ne. 28:21).

JOY AND EXALTATION

Joy is the best word to describe a continual state of exaltation. In
this sense, Lehi taught that Adam's fall brought about a condition in
which humankind could progress toward joy and achieve its result,
which is permanent exaltation. God brought us into this state of
mortality for this very purpose, and nothing less. The other kingdoms
of glory will experience happiness—that is, a state of well-being and
even of accomplishment—but they are barred forever from joy, for
there is no exaltation where they dwell.

A fulness of joy requires both the salvation of the body and spirit.
"For man is spirit. The elements are eternal, and spirit and element,
inseparably connected, receive a fulness of joy" (D&C 93:33). There
is a reason for this. The body brings its own dimension of accomplishment and enjoyment. Consider Joseph Smith's insight that "the
nearer man approaches perfection, the clearer are his views, and the
greater his enjoyments, till he has overcome the evils of his life and

lost every desire for sin."[33] What we have to understand is that we do not lose all desire, that both appetite and passion—perfected, enhanced, and growing out of the unity of the perfect spirit and the perfect body—remain with us always and become part of the fulness of our joy.

CONCLUSION

Gaining happiness, when the word is used as a synonym for joy, is the purpose of man's existence. However, happiness, when uncoupled from the element joy, is neither the purpose nor the meaning of existence. Happiness is an important aspect of existence, and the Lord desires us to strive to achieve it. He has even laid out the plan for us to do so. However, His plan for us goes well beyond achieving a state of well-being, which is sometimes mistakenly made synonymous with eternal life. Achieving a state of well-being is not our full purpose. Achieving eternal life is not an end in itself. The purpose of life—eternal life—is maintaining a state of joy. Now the question is, what does that mean and what method does God employ to bring that about? The answer to those questions will occupy the rest of this book.

CHAPTER 2

The INWARD FOUNTAIN of JOY

She came out of a colleague's office just as I was walking up the hall. The trace of tears was not fully masked by her quick half-smile in my direction. The hint of tears did not concern me at first. Those of us who work in religious education are familiar with them. Some come from joy or tenderness, some from sadness, some from frustration or disappointment; we see them often.

My colleague stood in his office doorway, watching her go. It was his look that caught me. I could see worry. "Not a good one?" I asked. "Not a good one," he confirmed. She was a young woman embarrassed by and estranged from her poor family. She was now in college, determined to make something of herself, yet failing.

"No hope?" I asked.

"There is always hope," he corrected, "if she will stay on the way. At least she's on the right step to begin."

"What step's that?" I enquired.

"Poor in spirit," he replied.

"That's a step?" I asked, with some surprise.

"Only if it brings her to Christ," he answered. "But if she will do that, then the other steps will lift her to the happiness and the fulfillment she seeks."

"Other steps?" I asked again.

"Yes," he said, "those outlined by the Savior in the Sermon on the Mount."

That was a new idea to me. I had always seen the Beatitudes as just statements about the reward for acquiring certain Christlike attributes. Progressive steps? Now that was an intriguing idea. So I investigated and discovered the following.

THE BEATITUDES: STEPS TO HAPPINESS

Surrounded by His most faithful disciples, the Lord gave what we call the Sermon on the Mount. In it, He taught us how to achieve blessedness, that "inward fountain of joy in the soul itself," as President Harold B. Lee called it.[1] In the gospels of Matthew and Luke, the Lord explains how one achieves a full measure of blessedness. In the context of His thought, blessedness denotes the security, assistance, and assurance that one receives when he has found favor with God.[2] In this light, the instructions in Matthew 5:3–12 really do become steps to securing a state of blessedness.

This discourse was so important that the Lord delivered it at least three times during His ministry: once on the mount above Galilee (as recorded in Matthew), once on the plains (as recorded by Luke), and once at Bountiful in America (as recorded by Mormon). Because of the fuller account given in the Book of Mormon, I will follow it while sharing additional insights from the biblical text.

The Words of the Twelve

According to Mormon's account, the Lord "stretched forth his hand unto the multitude, and cried unto them, saying: Blessed are ye if ye shall give heed unto the words of these twelve whom I have chosen from among you to minister unto you, and to be your servants" (3 Ne. 12:1). Clearly the first step toward blessedness is listening to and following those leaders whom the Lord has chosen and ordained for each age; they supply the direction and interpretation of the gospel as it applies to a particular period. In doing so, they show their listeners how to achieve happiness during that dispensation.

Baptism

The next step the Lord clearly stated with the words: "Blessed are ye if ye shall believe in me and be baptized, after that ye have seen me and know that I am" (3 Ne. 12:1). Then the Lord explains why: all those who show humility and are baptized "shall be visited with fire and with the Holy Ghost, and shall receive a remission of their sins" (3 Ne. 12:2). Entering into a covenant with the Lord becomes central to gaining the state of blessedness, because that is the only way we can receive the gift of the Holy Ghost. And, as we shall see, having that Spirit with us is absolutely critical to becoming more blessed.

The Poor in Spirit

In this context, when the Lord declared, "Yea, blessed are the poor in spirit who come unto me, for theirs is the kingdom of heaven" (3 Ne. 12:3), he was referring to those who lacked the gift of the Holy Ghost. For those whose spiritual lives have been less than they should be, either because they have extended no invitation to the Spirit, or because they have driven it away, there is hope.[3] If they will come to the Savior, He can bless them with the fire of everlasting life—but they must first come to Him.

Those who Mourn

After recognizing that we are poor in spirit, and that it is largely our own fault, the next step comes into play. The Lord promises, "Blessed are all they that mourn, for they shall be comforted" (3 Ne.12:4). The word mourn, in this context, carries the idea of grieving, but not necessarily out of bereavement or personal loss.[4] Rather, it is the sorrow which results from sin. In this light, consider the Lord's admonition to his disciples in America: "Ye shall offer for a sacrifice unto me a broken heart and a contrite spirit. And whoso cometh unto me with a broken heart and a contrite spirit, him will I baptize with fire and with the Holy Ghost" (3 Ne. 9:20). With deep repentance growing out of sincere sorrow for our sins, both those of commission and omission, we will find eternal life, and in this we will find comfort.

This promise of the Lord—that those who come to Him will find comfort—is especially interesting in light of an inference found in the same passage in Matthew (see 5:4). There the word "comfort" carries the broad meaning of admonishing, exhorting, entreating, and consoling, as well as comforting.[5] In these actions we see the work of the Holy Ghost, who is the First Comforter.

Modern revelation provides further interpretation of the Lord's full meaning. To Joseph Smith the Savior declared, "This is my gospel—repentance and baptism by water, and then cometh the baptism of fire and the Holy Ghost, even the Comforter, which showeth all things, and teacheth the peaceable things of the kingdom" (D&C 39:6). In this step to blessedness, the Lord promises His disciples that once they have repented and been baptized, they shall receive the gift of the Holy Ghost. This will bring them comfort, for they will have the richness of the Spirit in their lives. It will act to cleanse and purify their souls, burning out sin and dross by its fire.[6]

The Meek

The next step to blessedness comes to those who live so that the Holy Ghost directs and transforms them. The Lord said, "Blessed are the meek, for they shall inherit the earth" (3 Ne. 12:5). In the scriptural context, the meek are those who, due to the influence of the Spirit, place their full confidence and trust in the Lord.[7] Their gentle and mild disposition would rather take offense than give it; however, we must not view the meek as having no strength of character. These people are not cowards. They are courageous fighters for God's cause, but use spiritual weapons instead of the methods of the natural man. The absence of passion and wrath demonstrates their total self-control. It is because of this self-control that the Lord can bless them with the things of the earth. Though the Savior points the mind to eternal riches, we cannot overlook the fact that He may bless many of the meek with material rewards in mortality.

It is no surprise that the meek shall receive what many try but fail to grab for themselves: the goods of the earth. God can trust these who are masters of themselves to use material wealth the way He would have them. Jacob promised that those who seek first the kingdom of God and His righteousness and who "have obtained a hope in Christ . . . shall obtain riches, if ye seek them; and ye will seek them for the intent to do good—to clothe the naked, and to feed the hungry, and to liberate the captive, and administer relief to the sick and the afflicted" (Jacob 2:19). These are clearly meek acts.

Hungering and Thirsting After Righteousness

The next step toward blessedness builds on the actions associated with meekness. The Lord declared, "And blessed are all they who do hunger and thirst after righteousness, for they shall be filled with the Holy Ghost" (3 Ne. 12:6). The Savior's words paint a very strong picture. Hunger and thirst are driving forces. The Lord's metaphor stresses that the energy we exert to satisfy basic biological needs should also be applied to the spiritual. His thought also carries the idea of constancy: as the body must take daily nourishment, so must the spirit. Feeding the spirit through good works requires constant effort; daily deeds produce spiritual strengths.

I am reminded of Nephi, the son of Helaman, whose constant good works brought him to such a state of blessedness that the Lord entrusted him with the greatest powers ever given to mortal men. The Lord explained that the reason was because Nephi had "with unwearyingness declared the word, which I have given unto thee, unto this people. And thou hast not feared them, and hast not sought thine own life." The Lord went on, saying, "Now, because thou hast done this with such unwearyingness, behold, I will bless thee forever; and I will make thee mighty in word and in deed, in faith and in works" (Hel. 10:4–5). The Lord then promised him that he would "have power over this people, and shall smite the earth with famine, and with pestilence, and destruction, according to the wickedness of this people" (Hel. 10:6). Indeed, he would have power to move mountains and destroy buildings. (See Hel. 10:8–9.)

From Nephi's example, we see that hungering and thirsting after righteousness translates into unwearyingness in well-doing, and out of this activity grows access to godly power. Therefore, spiritual hunger does not derive simply from the lack of "food," as it does on the biological scale, but from the absence of the Spirit's tender touch. Once men and women have been touched by the Spirit and felt its sweetness, they desire both its constant companionship and the ever increasing ability it gives them to better serve others.

Thus, caring for our spirits through service to others (with the same fidelity we care for our physical bodies) opens the door to being "filled with the Holy Ghost." This appears to be a higher endowment than receiving the Comforter mentioned earlier. Modern revelation gives us a better understanding of what it means to be filled with the Spirit. Through the power of revelation, the Lord complimented some of his faithful modern Saints, saying that "I now send upon you another Comforter, even upon you my friends, that it may abide in your hearts, even the Holy Spirit of promise; which other Comforter is the same that I promised unto my disciples, as is recorded in the testimony of John. This Comforter is the promise which I give unto you of eternal life, even the glory of the celestial kingdom" (D&C 88:3-4).

The Book of Mormon explains what we must do to receive this promise. It says that we must "press forward with a steadfastness in Christ, having a perfect brightness of hope, and a love of God and of all men. Wherefore, if ye shall press forward, feasting upon the word of Christ, and endure to the end, behold, thus saith the Father: Ye shall have eternal life" (2 Ne. 31:20).

The Book of Mormon provides a number of examples of persons who followed this path and gained the assurance of eternal life. Lehi rejoiced that "the Lord hath redeemed my soul from hell; I have beheld his glory, and I am encircled about eternally in the arms of his love" (2 Ne. 1:15). To Alma, the Lord declared, "Thou art my servant; and I covenant with thee that thou shalt have eternal life; and thou shalt serve me and go forth in my name, and shalt gather together my sheep" (Mosiah 26:20). The Lord promised nine of his twelve Nephite disciples that "ye shall come unto me in my kingdom; and with me ye shall find rest" (3 Ne. 28:3). Other scriptures show the same power operating in our day. The Lord told Joseph Smith that "I am the Lord thy God, and will be with thee even unto the end of the world, and through all eternity; for verily I seal upon you your exaltation, and prepare a throne for you in the kingdom of my Father, with Abraham your father" (D&C 132:49).

He will give the same assurance to all who press forward with diligence in service, in love, and in hungering and thirsting after righteousness. The reason the Lord seals us His through this fulness of the work of the Spirit is because we have become "steadfast and immovable, always abounding in good works." This allows the Savior to "seal you his, that you may be brought to heaven, that ye may have everlasting salvation and eternal life, through the wisdom, and power, and justice, and mercy of him who created all things, in heaven and in earth, who is God above all" (Mosiah 5:15).

The Merciful

The Lord brings us to the next step of progression by saying, "Blessed are the merciful, for they shall obtain mercy" (3 Ne. 12:7).

Mercy follows naturally in the footsteps of meekness and of being filled with the Holy Ghost. As we have seen, meekness carries within it the element of self-control, of choosing to act in a godlike manner. Meek individuals hunger and thirst after righteousness and are therefore filled, through repentance, with the power of the Spirit. Mercy follows on the heels of meekness. It is a heartfelt ability that allows us to forgive those who trespass against us.

Matthew provides a more full understanding of what the Lord had in mind when He promised that the merciful should obtain mercy (Matt. 5:7). The word as used by Matthew comes out of a forensic setting, and comes into play only after a person has been found guilty. It describes a benevolent attitude on the part of the magistrate that is grounded on compassion so great that he refuses to punish the defendant, even though justice demands otherwise[8]. The idea, in its Christian context, denotes compassion for the guilty on the part of the offended. In this we see why mercy steps above and beyond meekness. It is one thing to act with restraint and grace toward others, and quite another to forgive them when they wrong us.

The Lord expressed the greatest example of mercy at the time He was being crucified. As Roman soldiers drove nails into His flesh, He asked the Father to forgive them. It is much easier to forgive others after time has dulled the pain they inflicted than it is to forgive the guilty even as they are executing the deed. The point we must not overlook in our example is that the soldiers were guilty of torturing and killing the Son of God. Yes, they were under orders, but orders cannot excuse evil deeds. Yes, they were subordinates, but subordination cannot justify heinous acts. Nevertheless, by the grace of Christ, applied as the evil deed was being done, these men will stand without condemnation for their participation in His crucifixion—forever. The Savior's act stands as the finest example of mercy.

Mercy often expresses itself in the form of grace. This dimension of mercy, in its ancient, nontheological sense, denoted kindness, favor, or goodwill of one toward another.[9] The Christians used grace to denote, among other things, the fond predisposition which God has for His children. God freely forgives and extends favor and love, which translates into assistance to those who are His. Though humankind sinned from the beginning, God has responded by giving us the Savior and the gospel. (See 1 Jn. 4:9-10.) This act of grace on His part opens the way to a fulness of joy.

The Father often expresses His grace by giving us the Holy Spirit. As the Spirit abides within us, we gain increased ability. This ability manifests itself in three ways: a loss of the propensity to sin; a greater capacity to love, forgive, and serve others; and, finally, a divine assurance of eternal life.

The Doctrine and Covenants helps us understand how this works. It tells us that the Savior did not receive "the fulness at the first, but received grace for grace," and that he went "from grace to grace" (D&C 93:12–14). To receive grace for grace is to receive divine assistance on the condition of giving assistance—but not just any kind of assistance on our part. What transforms assistance into grace is the kindness and favor felt by the giver toward the receiver.

God extended His grace to Jesus on condition of service. The scripture states specifically that the Lord received "grace *for* grace." When God extended His favor, the Son was obligated to do the same. As the Savior met this condition, God extended more grace to Him and He went from a lower level of grace to a higher. This cycle continued until the Son received a fulness of the glory of the Father. The implication of this is interesting. In a very real way, Christ himself was saved by grace.[10]

Because we have received of His grace, we too are obliged to serve, for grace carries with it the obligation to extend the same. The Savior has stated clearly that, "you shall receive grace for grace" if you want to "be glorified in me as I am in the Father" (D&C 93:20). If we meet the requirement by serving the Lord and magnifying what he has given us, we, like Christ, will "enter . . . into the joy of [our] lord" (Matt. 25:23).

The Pure in Heart

The next step toward full blessedness comes from the freedom bequeathed by meekness and mercy. As the Lord said, "Blessed are all the pure in heart, for they shall see God" (3 Ne. 12:8). The burdens of revenge, hatred, spite, and rancor make the heart both heavy and impure; meekness and mercy keep the heart soft and full of love. Those whose hearts have become hardened due to sin can only correct the situation by the awful means of having their hearts broken.

I find it interesting that it is the heart, not the brain or muscle, that determines whether one will see God and enter into true happiness. That is because the heart symbolizes our desires, or those things for which we yearn. The Savior's statement, "where your treasure is, there will your heart be also" (Matt. 6:21), shows that what we value determines our desires and wishes. Therefore, for those whose sights are set on blessedness, the condition of the heart is all important.

Some may think it is strange that greater stress is placed on desire than on deed, but the idea is correct on two counts. First, desire precedes deed. Where there is no desire, deeds remain undone, are done under coercion, or are done for the wrong reasons. Therefore, desire sanctifies deeds and makes them acceptable. Second, due to weakness, we are often unable to live up to the realization of our desires. Our spirit may be fully willing, but the flesh can be very weak. Though the Savior expects a willingness on our part to overcome all deficiency, He shows a willingness on His part to judge us initially on our desire to perform rather than our actual performance.

His willingness to judge us on desire is best illustrated in the sacramental blessing on the bread. There, those who partake covenant that "*they are willing* to take upon them the name of thy Son, and always remember him, and keep his commandments which he hath given them" (Moro. 4:3, italics added). Note that the partaker does not covenant to do all these things, but rather to demonstrate a constant willingness to do so. The end result of such sincere willingness is that "they may always have his Spirit to be with them" (Moro. 4:3). The point is that the Spirit comes according to our *willingness*, that is, according to our desire, not just according to our deeds. The reason the Lord does it this way is simple; it is only through His grace, expressed in the capacitating power of the Spirit, that God can transform our desires into deeds.

The condition which the heart must ultimately achieve is purity. The word "pure," found in Matthew, suggests not only a lack of defilement, but a state of refinement after fire has destroyed all dross and refuse.[11] In us, this is the work of the Holy Ghost as the baptism by fire. (See 2 Ne. 31:14–17.) Its purifying power prepares us to see

God. Joseph Smith taught that after "a person has faith in Christ, repents of his sins, and is baptized for the remission of his sins and receives the Holy Ghost, (by the laying on of hands), which is the first Comforter, then let him continue to humble himself before God, hungering and thirsting after righteousness, and living by every word of God, and the Lord will soon say unto him, Son, thou shalt be exalted."[12] Notice that receiving the promise of eternal life follows not long after a person hungers and thirsts after righteousness and expresses full, grace-assisted obedience. Having received the Father's promise of eternal life, the Prophet explained, a Saint can receive the Second Comforter. Indeed, he "will have the personage of Jesus Christ to attend him, or appear unto him from time to time."[13] The Prophet did not mention purity as a requirement, but the Savior did when He admonished the Saints to purify themselves "that your minds become single to God, and the days will come that you shall see him; for he will unveil his face unto you, and it shall be in his own time, and in his own way" (D&C 88:68).[14]

We must not overlook the fact that the Second Comforter, like the first, has a purpose in coming. Again we return to the Savior's teaching to His early apostles to find out what that purpose is. He told them, "If a man love me, he will keep my words: and my Father will love him, and we will come unto him, and make our abode with him" (John 14:23). Thus, the Second Comforter prepares us for full association with the Father. Speaking on this passage, the Prophet Joseph Smith confirmed that the Savior "will manifest the Father unto him [i.e., the disciple], and they will take up their abode with him, and the visions of the heavens will be opened unto him, and the Lord will teach him face to face, and he may have a perfect knowledge of the mysteries of the Kingdom of God."[15] All of this results from being pure.

The Peacemakers

A person who has arrived at such a high station will be an heir of all that God has, and thus the Savior brings us to the next step in blessedness. He says, "Blessed are all the peacemakers, for they shall be called the children of God" (3 Ne. 12:9). Isaiah called the Lord "the Prince of Peace" (Isa. 9:6). Under the inspiration of the Lord,

Zacharias, father of John the Baptist, prophesied of the coming Messiah, saying, "The dayspring [i.e., the Messiah] from on high hath visited us, To give light to them that sit in darkness and in the shadow of death, to guide our feet into the way of peace" (Luke 1:67, 78-79). The shepherds near Bethlehem heard the heavenly host proclaim, "Glory to God in the highest, and on earth peace, good will toward men" (Luke 2:14). Certainly the Savior came bringing peace to all the distraught and downhearted who would humble themselves and come to Him. He also left His peace, promising His disciples, "Peace I leave with you, my peace I give unto you: not as the world giveth, give I unto you. Let not your heart be troubled, neither let it be afraid" (John 14:27).

Through the Spirit, the pure become peacemakers, as was the Lord. They truly emulate this characteristic of their Father. Peacemaking pushes beyond mercy. Not only do the offended ones forgive, but they also seek reconciliation and oneness. Consider John's testimony concerning the willingness of the Father to bring us to Him. He states, "Herein is love, not that we loved God, but that he loved us, and sent his Son to be the propitiation for our sins" (1 John 4:10). God did not wait until we were sinless to bring about propitiation; he sent His Son first. The Savior does not demand righteousness at the first. While we are yet in our sins, we may accept or reject the atoning gift of His death.

The children of God act as did Jesus: they do not wait for the other to do right or to be good before they act. They strive to make reconciliation first. That is the real meaning of the golden rule: "Whatsoever ye would that men should do to you, do ye even so to them" (Matt. 7:12). These words teach us that it is the Christian's moral duty to give no less than he expects, and—this is important—it is the Saint's duty to give first.[16] God expects peacemaking to begin with His children.

The Persecuted

We are now reaching the last step to blessedness. This step carries a warning. The Savior cautions His disciples that as the world rejected His peace, it would likely reject theirs. We should carefully note His counsel: "blessed are all they who are persecuted for my name's sake, for theirs is the kingdom of heaven" (3 Ne. 12:10). The world will not love those who insist that peace can only come on those conditions laid down by the King of Peace. The world often builds mansions for those who would grind it under an iron heel while building crosses for those who love and would bring it peace. However, the Savior did not, nor will He ever, allow the threat of persecution to excuse us for failure to act. He has promised us all that He has. In return, He expects us to follow Him. He could not be more clear than when He said: "He that taketh not his cross, and followeth after me, is not worthy of me" (Matt. 10:38), and again, "If any man will come after me, let him deny himself, and take up his cross daily, and follow me" (Luke 9:23). Note that giving one's life once and for all is not the way salvation works; it is in daily forgiveness, daily reconciliation, and daily peacemaking that we follow the Savior.[17]

John the Revelator listed the sins of those who will suffer the second death, those banished from the face of Christ. These are "the fearful, and unbelieving, and the abominable, and murderers, and whoremongers, and sorcerers, and idolaters, and all liars" (Rev. 21:8). Many find it puzzling that cowards and the unfaithful are on a list that condemns those who commit the greatest of evils. Please note that they are not only on the list, but they head it. Many may admit that these are bad vices, but argue that placing them on the list of sins worthy of the second death seems too strong. Those who think this are overlooking the conditions that are facing the Saints in the last days. Now, as never before, Christ and Lucifer vie for the souls of humankind. This is a period in which opposition to goodness and virtue has and will continue to increase. Pressure continually mounts on the disciple to abandon the ways of God at the very time when valor becomes ever more necessary. Under such conditions, courage and faithfulness become supreme virtues. Those who abandon them turn their backs on the testimony of the Spirit and the power of grace, becoming cowards and disbelievers out of fear of the world. They will lose all.

Courage and faithfulness make the difference. The Lord reminds the disciple, "blessed are ye when men shall revile you and persecute, and shall say all manner of evil against you falsely, for my sake; For ye shall have great joy and be exceedingly glad, for great shall be your reward in heaven; for so persecuted they the prophets who were before you" (3 Ne. 12:11–12). Remember that the Lord does not promise the courageous great happiness in this life. There is good reason—persecution does not lend itself to happiness. But that is not to say that the Lord does not give just compensation. The faithful enjoy, even amidst their persecution, a blessed state; and in that they find joy.

CONCLUSION

All humankind exists that we might have joy. Of course, no one guarantees that we will achieve it. God, however, has carefully designed mortality to bring us joy if we follow the path that leads to it. Our task is to achieve blessedness—being one with Christ and God while we are here in mortality. The Lord presented His path to happiness in the Beatitudes. The path begins with coming to the Savior, repenting of our sins, and accepting His divine power to save. From there, we receive His grace, which assists us in becoming pure and reconciling ourselves to others. Finally, we become the children of God. God favors those who are valiant and He assures them of a place in heaven with Him. They are not freed from the stress and sorrow of mortality, but they do find peace in Christ and great joy.

It was months after my encounter with the teary-eyed young woman that I once again saw her visiting with my colleague. This time there were no tears. After she left, I inquired how she was doing.

"Fine," my friend reported.

"Stayed on the way?" I asked.

"Yes," he said.

"So which step is she on?" I queried.

"Beyond mourning, that's for sure," he replied with a smile, "But she's not on just one step. No one really progresses distinctly from one step to another. That's a nice model, but the reality is that one improves upon and benefits from lower steps while working on those higher. She is stretching all the way to peacemaking. She has reached out to her family, at last. I see a happy daughter of Christ emerging."

I was pleased, for I knew that out of her success would come a fulness of joy.

CHAPTER 3
JOY *and the* ATONEMENT

In the Book of Mormon, Lehi made it clear that Adam's fall brought mortal man into existence and that the purpose of that existence was for humankind to live in joy, both in mortality and in eternity. He went on to explain how God set up conditions to make this possible. He assured his son, Jacob, that:

> [T]he Messiah cometh in the fulness of time, that he may redeem the children of men from the fall. And because that they are redeemed from the fall they have become free forever, knowing good from evil; to act for themselves and not to be acted upon, save it be by the punishment of the law at the great and last day, according to the commandments which God hath given. Wherefore, men are free according to the flesh; and all things are given them which are expedient unto man. And they are free to choose liberty and eternal life, through the great Mediator of all men, or to choose captivity and death, according to the captivity and power of the devil (2 Ne. 2:26–27).

Because of the fall, all humankind possesses the ability to know good from evil. But the fall also could have left us spiritually dead—cut off from God and righteousness forever. The Savior redeemed us from the fall, but in so doing He did not make us righteous. Instead, He gave us the freedom to act for ourselves, which means that the consequences of our actions will bring us misery or joy. We must keep in mind what Alma explained:

Our first parents were cut off both temporally and spiritually from the presence of the Lord; and thus we see they became subjects to follow after their own will. Now behold, it was not expedient that man should be reclaimed from this temporal death, for that would destroy the great plan of happiness. Therefore, as the soul could never die, and the fall had brought upon all mankind a spiritual death as well as a temporal, that is, they were cut off from the presence of the Lord, it was expedient that mankind should be reclaimed from this spiritual death. Therefore, as they had become carnal, sensual, and devilish, by nature, this probationary state became a state for them to prepare; it became a preparatory state. And now remember, my son, if it were not for the plan of redemption, (laying it aside) as soon as they were dead their souls were miserable, being cut off from the presence of the Lord (Alma 42:7–11).

The fall placed humankind on the road to misery. The redemption opened up the road to joy. However, it only opened the road; we do not have to take it. The choice is completely up to us. What the redemption does is guarantee that if we obey, we will find joy. It was in this light that king Benjamin admonished his people to "consider on the blessed and happy state of those that keep the commandments of God. For behold, they are blessed in all things, both temporal and spiritual; and if they hold out faithful to the end they are received into heaven, that thereby they may dwell with God in a state of never-ending happiness" (Mosiah 2:41). Commandment-keeping, then, sets us on the road to temporal and spiritual happiness. The ultimate blessing, of course, hinges upon coming, once more, into God's presence—the redemption allows this to happen. Shortly before His death, the Savior explained to His disciples why He brought about the redemption.

THE SAVIOR'S POWER TO MAKE US ONE WITH GOD

Sitting with them at the Passover meal, the Lord filled the time instructing and foreshadowing. He wasted neither word nor deed during those last few anxious hours, and one statement among all the others promised hope and explanation. The Lord commanded these devoted men to "love one another, as I have loved you. Greater love hath no man than this, that a man lay down his life for his friends" (John 15:12–13). Just a few hours later, he would demonstrate His love's transcendence over a torturous death magnified by the pains of hellfire.[51] Though He was reluctant, love explained why He was willing and determined.

This necessary death opened up wonderful possibilities for His disciples. The Savior assured them that "ye are my friends, if ye do whatsoever I command you. Henceforth I call you not servants; for the servant knoweth not what his lord doeth: but I have called you friends; for all things that I have heard of my Father I have made known unto you" (John 15:15). Translated, "servant" can better be rendered as "slave" or "bondsman."[2] Because the Lord "hath purchased [the transgressor] with his own blood" (Acts 20:28) from the slave block of sin, He became that servant's rightful master.

Sin held humankind as slaves. We had no hope of self-redemption. We all faced the unmitigating powers of justice, which demanded eternal death as payment, but the Savior paid the price and bought us from sin. Paul referred to this when he asked, "Know ye not that . . . ye are not your own? For ye are bought with a price" (1 Cor. 6:19–20). The word "bought," which Paul chose to use, has strong theological implications. Greek religious law allowed a god to purchase an individual through his priests. The individual then became the property of the god and served him in his temple.[3] Paul's choice of this word plays upon this idea showing that the price Christ paid made us his "slaves." The leaders of the early Church were quite aware of this and often referred to themselves as the "slaves" (always translated as "servant" in the KJV) of Christ.[4]

However, as the Lord explained to His disciples, He did not shed His blood merely to take us from one kind of slavery—to sin—and put us in another, to Himself. He died to move us from bondage of any kind to full fellowship, if we choose to accept it.[5] Full fellowship takes four steps. First, as noted, the Redeemer buys us from the slavery of sin through shedding His blood and, thus, makes us His slaves. Second, through the power of spiritual adoption or rebirth, He frees us from His slavery and makes us His children. In this step, the humble and penitent are "born again; yea, born of God [that is, Christ], changed from their carnal and fallen state, to a state of righteousness, being redeemed of God, becoming his sons and daughters; And thus they become new creatures; and unless they do this, they can in nowise inherit the kingdom of God" (Mosiah 27:25–26). Those who do this, King Benjamin testifies, "shall be called the children of Christ, his sons, and his daughters" because they "are born of him" (Mosiah 5:7; see also Ether 3:14).

Third, as he promised His disciples, He elevates His children to the position of "friend." The word He used means a familiar associate, a companion, and more importantly, a confidante.[6] The power of grace reaches out to make disciples more than sons and daughters, raising them to the level of associates with Christ. On this level, the gift of the Second Comforter becomes available to them, and the Lord teaches them personally. In this way, "it is given unto many to know the mysteries of God," and to him who "will not harden his heart, to him is given the greater portion of the word, until it is given unto him to know the mysteries of God until he know them in full" (Alma 12:9–10). The Savior's promise to His disciples just hours before His death echoes this idea, as He tells them, "He that hath my commandments, and keepeth them, he it is that loveth me: and he that loveth me shall be loved of my Father, and I will love him, and will manifest myself to him" (John 14:21). At this time, the Lord will make "all things that I have heard of my Father" known (John 15:15), and the son or daughter becomes a friend and confidante.

Then comes the fourth step. Paul explained that "the Spirit itself beareth witness with our spirit, that we are the children of God [i.e. Elohim]: And if children, then heirs; heirs of God, and joint-heirs with Christ" (Rom. 8:16–17). In some inexplicable way, the Lord's blood raises us above the status of slaves to that of children—his children—and then to that of companions and confidantes and, finally, to equals and heirs.[7]

Amplifying Paul's point, Joseph Smith testified that "by him, and through him, and of him, the worlds are and were created, and the inhabitants thereof are begotten sons and daughters unto God" (D&C 76:24). With that in mind, consider the words of Elder Bruce R. McConkie:

Christ created worlds without number whose inhabitants are adopted into the family of God by the atoning sacrifice wrought on our earth. The faithful on all worlds are spiritually begotten in the same way as on our earth; they are begotten sons and daughters unto, not of, God.[8]

He explains further that the Savior

is the natural Son of God. But there is a system ordained whereby the rest of us can become sons of God. . . . Paul says that Christ is the Son and the Heir, and that we are joint-heirs . . . with Him. That is, if we are faithful, we are able to receive, possess, and inherit jointly with Him. . . . A joint heir inherits everything that the other heirs inherit. There is not a division so that one gets this and someone else gets another thing. All of them get the totality of the whole.[9]

Note that Elder McConkie said we become children *unto* Elohim. We already are the children *of* Elohim, but due to the fall and sin, we have forfeited that relationship. When the Savior restores it to us again, we become "children *unto* Elohim." Thus, like the Lord, we become heirs, not just through Him, but with Him, restored to full family relationship with the Father. So Paul testifies, "Wherefore thou art no more a servant, but a son; and if a son, then an heir of God through Christ" (Galatians 4:7).

To become the children of the Savior, we must repent, be baptized and receive the gift of the Holy Ghost. These ordinances also prepare us to become children unto Elohim. The next step, according to Elder McConkie, is celestial marriage:

[I]t opens the door to exaltation in the highest heaven of the celestial world. (See D&C 131:1–4.) And those who enter this order of matrimony and are faithful and true come up and inherit all things. (See D&C 76:50–70.) The terms and conditions of the oath and covenant of the priesthood say that those who magnify their callings receive all that our Father has. (See D&C 84:33–42.) They are joint-heirs; they are possessors of the whole. They have

inherited as their Prototype before inherited. They have the
fulness of glory and honor and dignity and dominion. And
so the members of the Church, who are the children of
Christ, who progress and advance and keep the commandments and are faithful and true, have the power to become
His brothers and sisters, to be joint-heirs with Him, to
receive, possess, and inherit the fulness of all good things,
and that is what the plan of salvation is all about.[10]

Keep in mind that the Savior's Atonement made all this possible, and
it came about only through the terrible agony which caused "God,
the greatest of all, to tremble because of pain, and to bleed at every
pore, and to suffer both body and spirit" (D&C 19:18).

THE SAVIOR DID NOT WANT TO DIE

Here I must emphasize that the Redeemer voluntarily submitted
to death. Allow me to expand the point by exploring a question. Did
the Savior have to endure the spiritual agony which racked Him in
Gethsemane or the brutal physical torture inflicted by the scourge
whip and the cross? Consider for a moment that there was no fence
around the garden to lock Him in, no shackles to keep Him fettered,
no gate that opened only inward. Those puny nails which pinned Him
to the cross were no match for power of the one who made the Red
Sea part and the winds and waves of the Galilean sea cease and be still.
In the garden, He had the full power both of His godhood and of His
agency. No number of temple guards or Jewish magistrates could have
arrested Him against His will. His statement to Peter at the moment of
His arrest, "thinkest thou that I cannot now pray to my Father, and he
shall presently give me more than twelve legions of angels" (Matt.
26:53), was not hyperbole but a statement of terrific fact.

Remember, too, that He did not want to stay in the garden; He
did not want to endure the suffering of the damned, the breadth,
height, and depth of which swept over Him fully and completely. One
feels the anguish in His plea to His disciples, "My soul is exceeding
sorrowful, even unto death; tarry ye here and watch" (JST, Mark
14:38). As they did so, their sympathy swelled and they rejoined, "The

spirit truly is ready, but the flesh is weak" (Mark 14:38). They sensed the deep aversion in the Lord's mortal body as it resisted the immense torture that would prove to be simply the first light touch of an indescribable agony that would cause Him, God, to sweat blood.

We sometimes forget that He had to stay in the garden and on the cross without incentive or assistance from others, even from His Father.[11] Brigham Young understood this. He testified to the Saints that the greater the vision and power one has, the more God will test that individual to see if he will keep his covenants.

> And when such individuals are off their guard they are left to themselves, as Jesus was. For this express purpose the Father withdrew His spirit from His son, at the time He was to be crucified. Jesus had been with His Father, talked with Him, dwelt in His bosom, and knew all about heaven, about making the earth, about the transgression of man, and what would redeem the people, and that He was the character who was to redeem the sons of earth, and the earth itself from all sin that had come upon it. The light, knowledge, power, and glory with which He was clothed were far above, or exceeded that of all others who had been upon the earth after the fall, consequently at the very moment, at the hour when the crisis came for Him to offer up His life, the Father withdrew Himself, withdrew His Spirit, and cast a vail [sic] over Him. That is what made Him sweat blood. If He had had the power of God upon him, He would not have sweat blood; but all was withdrawn from Him, and a veil was cast over Him, and He then plead with the Father not to forsake Him. "No," says the Father, "you must have your trials, as well as others."[12]

It is interesting that Brigham Young says the test comes when people are off their guard. Could this have happened to the Lord? That may seem unlikely since, only some six months before, He had held counsel with angels over this very matter. At that time, "there talked with him two men, which were Moses and Elias: Who appeared in glory, and spake of his decease which he should accomplish at Jerusalem" (Luke 9:30–31). However, it was one thing, on the Lord's part, to plan for His coming death, and quite another to die.

Apparently, the Father did not reveal the full cost and weight of the Atonement until the moment the Son entered into its throes. In this light we can understand a little detail supplied by Mark. He noted that the Savior and his disciples "came to a place which was named Gethsemane: and he saith to his disciples, Sit ye here, while I shall pray. And he taketh with him Peter and James and John, and began to be sore amazed, and to be very heavy" (Mark 14:32–33).[13] A more literal translation would read, He "began to be greatly astonished, and to be distressed."[14] Then the moment came when the full weight bore down on Him. Out of this revelation came His cry, "My soul is exceeding sorrowful, even unto death" (Matthew 26:38). Expanding this thought, Elder Maxwell testified that:

> [W]hen the unimaginable burden began to weigh upon Christ, it confirmed His long-held and intellectually clear understanding as to what He must now do. His working through began, and Jesus declared: "Now is my soul troubled; and what shall I say? Father, save me from this hour." Then, whether in spiritual soliloquy or by way of instruction to those about Him, He observed, "But for this cause came I unto this hour" (John 12:27).

> Later, in Gethsemane, the suffering Jesus began to be "sore amazed" (Mark 14:33), or, in the Greek, "awestruck" and "astonished."

> Imagine, Jehovah, the Creator of this and other worlds, "astonished"! Jesus knew cognitively what He must do, but not experientially. He had never personally known the exquisite and exacting process of an atonement before. Thus, when the agony came in its fulness, it was so much, much worse than even He with his unique intellect had ever imagined! No wonder an angel appeared to strengthen Him! (See Luke 22:43.)

> The cumulative weight of all mortal sins—past, present, and future—pressed upon that perfect, sinless, and sensitive Soul! All our infirmities and sicknesses were somehow, too, a part of the awful arithmetic of the Atonement.[15]

Again, let me stress, His agency allowed Him to back away, walk out, decide the cost was too great and leave both garden and cross behind Him. His statement to Peter that He could count on legions of angels to help Him accomplish His desire opens some interesting possibilities, but none were ever realized. The historical reality is that He had made His choice eons ago when, in the premortal existence He proclaimed, "Father, thy will be done, and the glory be thine forever" (Moses 4:2). From that point on, there was no turning back, no decision that had to be remade. The Son had given His word, and that word would stand without reconsideration. The foreknowledge of God decreed that the Son would keep His covenant, and on that condition, He armed the Son with the power and station of a God possessing life in Himself. Therefore, God mustered no angels; He did not have twelve legions of seraphs standing by. No one in heaven, recalling their support of His cause as Savior, stood in that critical moment anxiously wondering what the Son would do. He moved according to His promise and His Father's will, and refused to leave the unguarded garden.

It seems true that His eternal life was contingent on fulfilling the covenant He had made with the Father, a covenant that included the Atonement. Therefore, the Atonement was necessary even for the salvation of the Son. At the same time He died for others, He kept the covenant and saved Himself. Even though that is the case, one thing seems very evident from the record: saving Himself was not His primary motivation. In fact, it may not have motivated Him at all. The only thing we know for sure is that He did what He did for love, for He did indeed lay His life down for His friends.

Therefore, His love bound Him to the garden and pinned Him to the cross—a love stronger than any chain ever forged or any spike ever shaped. He stayed not for Himself, but for others—for us—and staying proved through exquisite fire the breadth of His love for us all. Knowing what His love cost Him, we should love Him all the more. The Atonement grew out of love so that love would grow out of appreciation for the Atonement.

THE COST OF SIN

We can better appreciate what the Lord's love did for us if we understand what would have happened without it. Paul said, "The wages of sin is death" (Rom. 6:23). It is interesting that he did not say, "the wages of sin is hell." We often pit heaven against hell, but we miss an important point when we do. Of course, hell will claim some: "sorcerers, and adulterers, and whoremongers, and whosoever loves and makes a lie" (D&C 76:103), but even "they shall be heirs of salvation" (D&C 76:88)—which the telestial kingdom is, in part—after their sins are purged. No, it is not hell we need ultimately fear; it is death—specifically spiritual death. Spiritual death means being banished from God's presence forever, being "the only ones on whom the second death shall have any power; Yea, verily, the only ones who shall not be redeemed in the due time of the Lord, after the sufferings of his wrath"(D&C 76:37–38). Some form of this death, so far as they have failed to become like God, even applies to those in the highest degree of the terrestrial kingdom.

Now under God's law, the only way to avoid spiritual death is not to sin. If we live perfectly, then we shall be justified in the eyes of His law and we can return to live with God forever. Unfortunately, that brute force approach will not work for us, because, as Paul says, "all have sinned, and come short of the glory of God" (Rom. 3:23).

Some people try to get around this by believing that little sins really don't matter; they rationalize that only big sins really hurt us. What I must make clear is that according to God's law, one little sin is all it takes to put us under the power of eternal death. Remember that Paul did not separate sin into two categories: big ones that hurt us and little ones that don't. When it comes to spiritual death, any sin will destroy us. The reason is quite simple. The Lord informs us that "unto every kingdom is given a law" (D&C 88:38). Note, He did not say "laws;" He said "law"—only one. He tells us further, "There is a law, irrevocably decreed in heaven before the foundations of this world, upon which all blessings are predicated" (D&C 130:20). Again, He confirms that there is only one law, at least from His eternal perspective. Emphasizing the point, the Savior states: "Behold, mine house is a house of order . . . and not a house of confusion. Will I accept of an offering . . . that is not made in my name? Or will I receive at your hands that which I have not appointed? And will I appoint unto you . . . except it be by law, even as I and my Father ordained unto you, before the world was?" (D&C 132:8–11). The Father and Son ordained that by law (not laws) we would be blessed. They set it in cement before the world was, and left no chance that They would revoke it later on.

That law defines what we must do to inherit eternal life. According to Alma, God's law had two components to it. In his words, there was a punishment affixed to the law "which also was eternal as the life of the soul." This was balanced opposite what he calls "the plan of happiness," or, in other words, the reward "which was as eternal also as the life of the soul" (Alma 42:16).

The reward of eternal happiness, however, could come only on condition of perfection. When we do not fulfill that condition, sad consequences follow. The slightest imperfection meant that "all mankind were fallen, and they were in the grasp of justice; yea, the justice of God, which consigned them forever to be cut off from his presence." Now, this law plays a big part in one's predicament because "How could he sin if there was no law? How could there be a law save there was a punishment? Now, there was a punishment affixed, and a just law given" (Alma 42:14, 17–18).

The problem comes from the fact that we must obey perfectly the law of God. That means we either keep the whole law or we break the whole law. This is where things get sticky. If we keep the law, then we keep it 100 percent. Since it is a just law, keeping it means that we receive 100 percent of the reward. The reward is eternal life, to live with the Father and Son forevermore. Conversely, when we break the law, since there is only one, we break 100 percent of it. James said it best: "For whosoever shall keep the whole law, and yet offend in one point, he is guilty of all" (James 2:10). Either we keep the law or we don't. If we don't, then we have broken the whole law, and receive the whole punishment. The punishment is eternal death.

The implications are even more frightening. Jacob testified to his people that "our spirits must become subject to that angel who fell from before the presence of the Eternal God, and became the devil, to rise no more. And our spirits must have become like unto him, and we become devils, angels to a devil, to be shut out from the presence of our God, and to remain with the father of lies, in misery, like unto himself" (2 Ne. 9:8–9). Remember, a single little sin will put us in this situation just as completely as a big sin. To illustrate, consider the following parable.

THE PARABLE OF THE FIVE HUNDRED PENNIES

A story is told of a little orphan boy who really wanted to go to the circus. The cost, he discovered, was five dollars. By working hard all summer, he earned 500 pennies, just enough to get him into the show. Delighted with the prospects, he walked from the orphanage to the fairgrounds in full anticipation of a good time.

As he entered the gate, he could barely see the booth where they sold tickets to the "Greatest Show Ever." Its beckoning light reached as far as the gate, but just barely. He hadn't realized the walk would be quite so long. The goal lay at the end of the Way—a straight and narrow path that would take him where he wanted to go. A dim but ever steady light was there to guide him. All he had to do was stay on the Way.

He soon discovered, however, that there were other paths and another way. It was called the Midway. He knew it was there. He had been warned about it, the place where little boys and little girls can wander, even get lost, and worse, forget—forget about the circus; a place where they can spend pennies, lots and lots of pennies and nickels and dimes and, especially, dollars. In fact, the Midway accepts anything they take at the ticket booth, and the Midway comes first.

This little boy, however, was determined and kept his eyes on his goal and made good progress. But then temptation came. He had just about come to the end of the Way. There was only one more stand to go, there where the Way and the Midway brush for the last time. He smelled delicious aromas long before he got to the stand; lovely, sweet smells wafting from its ovens. This stand sparkled clean and white with a lovely, absolutely spotless, display case. Our little boy sniffed the luscious scent, and, overwhelmed by the savor, walked into the store, just to see.

There, among other confections, he discovered wonderful lollipops, and for only one little penny. Would one penny really matter? He took one from his pocket and it did not feel any lighter. So, he decided the gamble was worth it and bought the sucker, and it was wonderful.

Back onto the Way, he quickly covered the distance to where they sell the tickets to the greatest show on earth. There he was greeted by a kindly man who readily accepted the boy's change. For a moment the boy thought all would be well, until the man began counting the pennies. The boy's heart sank. Sure enough, the man soon pointed out that the boy was a penny short. The gate keeper explained that he could give the boy a ticket only if he came up with that last penny. Did he not have someone he could turn to, someone who could help him? No, unfortunately, he had no one.

So, here at the very end of summer he had forfeited all. And in that realization, the lollipop's sweetness turned horribly bitter, and a tear stung the little boy's cheek.

THE NEED FOR A REDEEMER

Now what is the point of this sad story? As I said at the beginning, it's to illustrate a point: "The wages of sin is death" (Rom. 6:23), not just big sins, but little sins as well. In fact one little sin, as I said, will do the job nicely. And the real clincher is that we can't do a thing to erase it. What's more, there is nothing anyone else can do to erase it, either. It remains forever. The penny is gone, and no one can ever get it back.

So should we just give up? Is there no hope? There is none if we try to save ourselves. But the joy growing out of the Atonement is that we do not have to save ourselves. The Lord can save us, if we will let Him.

What does it take? We, like the little boy in the parable, must find someone who can make up for our loss and foolishness. The scriptures teach us that such a one must be our Father. In other words, once we have sinned and thus lost our station in the family, we must get back into it. According to John, that is what the Savior was telling Nicodemus when he came to Jesus and initiated the following conversation:

> Rabbi, we know that thou art a teacher come from God: for no man can do these miracles that thou doest, except God be with him. Jesus answered and said unto him, Verily, verily, I say unto thee, Except a man be born again, he cannot see the kingdom of God. Nicodemus saith unto him, How can a man be born when he is old? can he enter the second time into his mother's womb, and be born? Jesus answered, Verily, verily, I say unto thee, Except a man be born of water and of the Spirit, he cannot enter into the kingdom of God. That which is born of the flesh is flesh; and that which is born of the Spirit is spirit. Marvel not that I said unto thee, Ye must be born again (John 3:2–7).

The imagery of rebirth as the means of entering the kingdom of heaven is as old as Adam. An angel explained to him,

> That by reason of transgression cometh the fall, which fall bringeth death, and inasmuch as ye were born into the world by water, and blood, and the spirit, which I have made, and so became of dust a living soul, even so ye must be born again into the kingdom of heaven, of water, and of the Spirit, and be cleansed by blood, even the blood of mine Only Begotten; that ye might be sanctified from all sin, and enjoy the words of eternal life in this world, and eternal life in the world to come, even immortal glory (Moses 6:59).

The Book of Mormon stresses the idea. As Alma taught, all must be born again as the Savior's sons and daughters (Mosiah 27:25–26). They must be "redeemed from the fall" and brought back into God's presence (Ether 3:13).

Now to understand why we can be saved through the power of rebirth, let us again return to our parable.

THE MAN AND THE LITTLE BOY

Seeing the boy's tears, the gatekeeper asked how badly the boy wanted to see the show. The little boy expressed his keen desire. The man then said that there might be a way. He acknowledged knowing that the little boy was an orphan, and explained that if the little boy were willing to be the gatekeeper's son, he could help him. The little boy wanted to know how. The man explained that the owner of the circus had once asked him to do something very hard. Though he feared he might not be able to, he succeeded and in the process earned a lot of pennies. If the boy would become his son, he explained, then he could give him a penny. The result would be wonderful. First, the owner of the circus would get what he wanted, five dollars; second, the good man would get what he wanted, a son; and, third, the boy would get double because he would get a ticket and a father.

The boy thought about all this for a moment and then asked if there was a catch. The good man replied there was, the lollipop. The little boy became even more conscious of the lollipop. He didn't like it anymore. Yet somehow part of him did not want to give it up. The good man explained that it was the boy's choice—he could not force him. With some courage, the little boy finally took it out of his mouth and handed it to the good man. With that, the gatekeeper dropped a penny into the pile, pulled the pennies into a drawer, took a ticket and came out of the cage, and father and son took hands and walked together to see the wonder of the circus.

But wait. The scene isn't quite over. Did you catch it? The motion was not exaggerated, but definite, just there where they passed the trash can. The good man threw away, with vehemence, the lollipop. Do you wonder why? You see, he hates lollipops, for suckers destroy little boys and little girls.

But why, you may ask, if he was only going to destroy the lollipop, did he ask it of the little boy? It was because the little boy had to make a decision. Did he want a lollipop, or did he want a father? He chose a father, and life.

CONCLUSION

Adam fell that humankind might live. Christ died that humankind might live eternally. His grace provides the way. I want to emphasize that point; otherwise, my story may cause some to draw wrong conclusions. They may decide that the good man really did very little for the boy, merely paying 1/500th of the necessary price. Not so! Though the little boy managed to make it through the Midway with 499 pennies, he still could not get into the circus. He was saved by grace *after* all he could do, or, to say it better, he was saved by grace *apart* from all he could do.[16] He did his absolute best and STILL FAILED. Keeping 499 pennies did not save him. That one penny, given with love, did.

I fear that by saying that, you could draw the wrong conclusion. You could decide that the Lord's Atonement only covers that portion of the salvation requirements we are not able to complete ourselves. Some of our detractors describe Mormonism as the "religion of the gaps." What they mean is that we view the role of Jesus as filling up the gap between how close each one of us comes to salvation and what is actually needed. For example, if a Saint does his best but can only get 10 percent of the way to salvation, Jesus fills in the 90 percent gap. Conversely, if the Saint does 90 percent, then Jesus only need fill in a 10 percent gap.

I know a lot of Saints that ascribe to this mistaken view. Because the Lord requires us to enter into covenant with him and strive to keep His commandments, they have erroneously concluded that they are doing it to earn, at least partially, their way into heaven. We are not. We can't earn our way into heaven.

So why the commandments? God made them as our way of showing our acceptance of the Savior's grace. We can't earn salvation, but by striving to obey, we show our acceptance of His grace through which salvation comes. That is what the little boy did—he accepted the good man's gift. It was his accepting the gift, not the number of pennies the boy kept or that the gatekeeper had to put in the pile, that gave the little boy his reward.

The Book of Mormon could not be more clear when it says, "it is only in and through the grace of God that ye are saved" (2 Ne. 10:24). Joseph Smith changed Romans 3:24 from reading that we are "justified *freely* by his grace through the redemption that is in Christ Jesus," to read we are "justified *only* by his grace through the redemption that is in Christ Jesus" (italics added).

Another incorrect conclusion someone could draw is that the person who sins little adds but little to the Savior's suffering, thereby costing the Savior little in the redemptive process. The truth of the matter is, the Savior did not suffer for a finite amount of sin. He suffered to meet the dictates of an eternal and demanding law. He assures us that we have no idea of the depth of His suffering: "how sore you know not, how exquisite you know not, yea, how hard to bear you know not" (D&C 19:15). We do know that it caused this God, "the greatest of all, to tremble because of pain, and to bleed at every pore, and to suffer both body and spirit" (v. 18), and that through it he "descended below all things" (D&C 88:6). Therefore, whether we sin a little or a lot, we neither add to nor take away from what the Savior had to endure. He, unlike us, had to keep the *whole* law, yet pay for offense against the *whole* law.

Some may feel that this makes the Atonement impersonal, that Jesus did not die for us, or better, that He did not die for "me." That is not the case. The Atonement was personal. He did die for each of us. Consider Abinadi's testimony: "Behold, I say unto you, that when his soul has been made an offering for sin he shall see his seed" (Mosiah 15:10). Part of the marvel of the Atonement is its personal nature. Jesus was somehow able to see those who would accept His sacrifice, and more, He was able to accept them as His own. (See Mosiah 15:11.)

The point is that the Lord died to save us all and His mercy can too, but He will not save us against our will. He assures us that everyone who "breaketh a law, and abideth not by law, but seeketh to become a law unto itself, and willeth to abide in sin, and altogether abideth in sin, cannot be sanctified by law, neither by mercy, justice, nor judgment. Therefore, they must remain filthy still" (D&C 88:35). Why? They will not accept the Lord's cleansing and saving grace. Note that He does not withdraw it, but they will not accept it. He will not save them in their sins (see Alma 11:34–37).

We show our acceptance of His grace through faith, repentance, baptism, receiving the gift of the Holy Ghost, and striving to do His will. By accepting His grace through such faithfulness, we become cleansed from sin. "Therefore," Paul testified, "being justified by faith, we have peace with God through our Lord Jesus Christ: By whom also we have access by faith into this grace wherein we stand, and rejoice in hope of the glory of God" (Rom. 5:1–2). Note that by our faithfulness we access His grace, out of which we "rejoice in hope of the glory of God." The Atonement is the good news by which we rejoice in this life and have admittance to joy in the life to come.

CHAPTER 4
LOVE *and* JOY

Caught up in vision, the prophet Lehi traversed a dark and fearful waste. After many hours, in near despair, he cried out for the Lord to save him. Immediately he stood before a large and spacious field full of streams and rivulets, roads and trails, people of all kinds, and overshadowed by an immense building. The building, however, did not grab his attention. What did was a tree unlike any he had seen. Its beauty beckoned him. He responded and moved toward it. He sensed that its "fruit was desirable to make one happy," and when he partook of it, he found that "it was most sweet, above all that I ever before tasted. Yea, and I beheld that the fruit thereof was white, to exceed all the whiteness that I had ever seen. And as I partook of the fruit thereof it filled my soul with exceedingly great joy" (1 Ne. 8:10–12).

THE TREE IN LEHI'S DREAM

As vivid and real as Lehi's experience seemed, the tree did not actually exist. The Lord was teaching His prophet through symbols and images. He used the tree and its fruit as types of things that, when they touched and became a part of Lehi, brought him a fulness of joy.

Lehi told his children about his dream and gave them a partial interpretation, but left them to ponder its full meaning. The vision seemed to fascinate all who heard it. Heated debate followed; Nephi tells us that his brothers disputed "one with another concerning the things which my father had spoken unto them." Nephi was sympathetic with their difficulty, confessing that Lehi "truly spake many great things unto them, which were hard to be understood" (1 Ne. 15:2–3). Unlike his brothers, however, who wanted to solve the problem with logic instead of Spirit, Nephi used humility. He understood that one could not know the meaning of these things "save a man should inquire of the Lord" (1 Ne. 15:3), which he did.

The Spirit of the Lord caught him up into the mountain of revelation for instruction. Nephi reports that "the Spirit said unto me: Behold, what desirest thou? And I said: I desire to behold the things which my father saw. And the Spirit said unto me: Believest thou that thy father saw the tree of which he hath spoken?" (1 Ne. 11:2-4). It is interesting that of all the elements in Lehi's dream, the Spirit focused only on the tree, and kept the focus there. Gaining Nephi's commitment of faithfulness, the Spirit promised Nephi that:

> [T]hou shalt behold the things which thou hast desired. And behold this thing shall be given unto thee for a sign, that after thou hast beheld the tree which bore the fruit which thy father tasted, thou shalt also behold a man descending out of heaven, and him shall ye witness; and after ye have witnessed him ye shall bear record that it is the Son of God. And it came to pass that the Spirit said unto me: Look! And I looked and beheld a tree; and it was like unto the tree which my father had seen; and the beauty thereof was far beyond, yea, exceeding of all beauty; and the whiteness thereof did exceed the whiteness of the driven snow (1 Ne. 11:6–8).

The tree stood alone on the Spirit's stage, but even with no other objects cluttering the scene, Nephi could not guess its meaning. Therefore, he asked the Spirit if he might "know the interpretation thereof" (1 Ne. 11:11). The Spirit did not answer directly, but rather opened another vision to Nephi, one revealing Mary alone and then with the infant Savior. When this portion of the vision closed, an angel, not the Spirit, took over. The angel asked the apt student, "Knowest thou the meaning of the tree which thy father saw?" (v. 21). It is interesting that with only this much of a hint, Nephi had it figured out: "Yea, it is the love of God, which sheddeth itself abroad

in the hearts of the children of men; wherefore, it is the most desirable above all things" (v. 22). The angel responded, amplifying, "Yea,
and the most joyous to the soul" (v. 23).

How did the vision Nephi saw lead him to the correct interpretation of Lehi's tree? Nephi seems to have been under the same spiritual
influence as John, the Apostle, who testified, "For God so loved the
world, that he gave his only begotten Son, that whosoever believeth
in him should not perish, but have everlasting life" (John 3:16).
Christ, and salvation through Him, is the supreme love-gift of God,
and the tree represented that gift.

GOD IS LOVE

The angel made it perfectly clear to Nephi that the child born of
Mary was "the Son of God, after the manner of the flesh" (1 Ne.
11:18). In order to underscore the point, "the angel said unto me:
Behold the Lamb of God, yea, even the Son of the Eternal Father!" (v.
21). Again, Nephi and John seem to have understood the same
message. John testified that "God is love. In this was manifested the
love of God toward us, because that God sent his only begotten Son
into the world, that we might live through him. Herein is love, not
that we loved God, but that he loved us, and sent his Son to be the
propitiation for our sins" (1 Jn. 4:8–10).

John's point is that God expressed His love toward humankind in
two ways: He acted first, before we as mortals loved Him, and He
gave us His only begotten Son. God's love waited neither for righteousness nor reciprocation. It responded to our need, giving us what
we desperately needed: a redeemer as a propitiation.

The Greek word translated as "propitiation" can also be rendered
"expiation."[1] It means to make complete satisfaction in behalf of
another. The idea behind the word is conciliation through which two
objectives are accomplished: first, the offended party is appeased, and
second, the guilty party regains favorable status with him.[2] True expiation must do both. If an arbiter only accomplishes appeasement
between estranged parties, unity and fellowship may not follow. A
propitiator must go beyond simple mediation by uniting the offender
with the offended in friendship. So the Savior, as our propitiation,

came not only to appease the demands of justice but also to bring us into favor with God. In this we see God's objective in giving us His love-gift first: He wanted His children to recognize the value of His gift and to respond, in turn, with love born of appreciation.

God seems to have had two major objectives in giving us His Son. First, it was a means of gaining the love of the faithful. Second, it made life possible *through* the Son, as John insists. One aspect of God's love expresses itself in His desire that we gain eternal life. As we have learned, gaining eternal life means obtaining a fulness of joy. We can only do this as we overcome the natural man, and are born again, "sanctified from all sin, and enjoy the words of eternal life in this world, and eternal life in the world to come, even immortal glory" (Moses 6:59). All this comes through the propitiation of the Savior. That is, He makes our eternal joy possible, and we live through Him. (See John 17:13.)

POWER TO BECOME THE CHILDREN OF GOD

John understood the indispensable role played by God's love-gift to His children. He bore witness that "as many as received him, to them gave he power to become the sons [and daughters] of God, even to them that believe on his name: Which were born, not of blood, nor of the will of the flesh, nor of the will of man, but of God" (John 1:12–13).

John emphasizes that it takes power to overcome our fallen natures, find reconciliation with the Father, and be born again. To better understand John's idea, we must turn to an insight not captured in the King James translation of the Greek text. The Apostle did not use the Greek word most often translated in the Bible as "power," but one that is better translated as "authority," though English definitions do not exactly fit.[3] I will define them with their New Testament nuances and then capitalize the English word to remind us of these nuances.

The difference in meaning between the two words is important.[4] The word Power suggests external force or potency, while Authority suggests inner power controlled by the individual. With the Savior, the word underscores His divinely appointed ability to act for God. It stresses the right He has to perform the Father's will "to bring to pass the immortality and eternal life of man" (Moses 1:39). Therefore, Authority is a good translation.[5]

We should also understand the force of the word Authority in its judicial sense, which is the right to decide cases. It defines God's right to choose to whom He will and will not extend Power and give Authority. When the Savior decides for a person, He uses His authority to make the recipient a child of God, the gift of the Holy Ghost is then bestowed, and the individual is born again into the divine family.

Let me emphasize that, in the process, the Lord bequeaths His own Authority on the individual.[6] This power, abiding within the soul, makes it possible for the daughter or son of Christ to walk in the ways of the Lord. Thus, John states, "Whosoever is born of God doth not continue in sin; for the Spirit of God remaineth in him; and he cannot continue in sin, because he is born of God, having received that holy Spirit of promise" (JST, 1 Jn. 3:9). John further affirms, "We know that whosoever is born of God continueth not in sin; but he that is begotten of God and keepeth himself, that wicked one overcometh him not" (JST, 1 Jn. 5:18). The word translated "keepeth" means "to protect" or "to guard."[7] Now, just because the Saint has been born of God does not mean he cannot fall.[8] However, as John notes, the true disciple, being filled with love, takes care to protect himself and never let down his guard.

Returning to John's statement that those who are touched by God's love are "born, not of blood, nor of the will of the flesh, nor of the will of man, but of God" (John 1:13), we see that it is neither mortal desire nor physical passion that allows this process to take place. Rather, it is the disposition of, and a dispensation from, God. Thus, to rephrase John 1:12–13, the Savior extends His Authority, the saving power that abides in Him, to the believing individual. By the Lord's Authority, the individual becomes a child of God. John stresses that it is God's grace, not the individual's will or desire or passion, which brings this about. God sets the terms of salvation as an expression of His Authority alone.

Let me stress one point: the Power to become a child of Christ does not abide in us. We cannot of ourselves decide to become the sons and daughters of God and then do it. It takes something more than we have. Because of His propitiation, the Savior can grant us what we lack: Power. He grants that Power on the basis of our faith and determination to accept and follow Him. This gift is a manifestation of His love.

THE WOMAN WITH THE ISSUE OF BLOOD

Mark tells us of an incident in the Lord's ministry with succinct sensitivity that illustrates the point (see Mark 5:25–34).[9] He explains that a certain woman suffered from an issue of blood for twelve years. If this was associated with menses, as it seems to have been, then she had never been free from a bloody flux since she was eleven or twelve. That would have made her about twenty-five at the time of the event Mark reports.

Such a malady would have imposed great cultural burdens upon her. It meant that she was in a state of continual ceremonial uncleanliness.[10] Because of this, the regulations of the day forbade her from entering the synagogue or temple. Further, she could never marry, for her touch would make her husband unclean as well. Simply put, the malady deprived her of both marriage and motherhood. Thus, the disease closed to her much that women of that time period desired. It is little wonder that she spent all she had on physicians, hoping that they could cure her. To her disappointment and dismay, they only made the condition worse, perhaps even life threatening.

Then she heard about a rabbi from Galilee whom some proclaimed as the Messiah. Reports came of his ability to heal and give comfort. She listened and believed. Over time her faith grew, and with it her determination. He could heal her, she was sure. But there was a problem; she was unclean. How could she approach the Messiah? She mistakenly believed that if she touched Him or if He knowingly touched her, the very touch would make Him unclean, a state in which a holy man must never find himself. Even so, she felt she could be healed only by His touch. Luckily, there was a way for her to get around the difficulty. If He did not knowingly touch her, according to the law, His innocence would guard him from uncleanliness.[11] All she had to do was touch Him without His knowledge, then He would still be clean and she would be whole.

So she traveled, according to tradition,[12] from her home in Caesarea Philippi to the northwestern shore of the Galilee, some twenty-five miles to where the Savior was ministering. A throng of disciples and interested people followed Him. It was not hard for her to get in close, and, at the right moment, reach through the crowd and touch His robe, and then allow the throng to surround her.

But why touch the robe? A blue ribbon bound the hem of the male outer garment reminding the wearer that he was under a holy covenant with God.[13] For this reason, the robe was considered sacred. The covenant it represented reached back to Abraham and the Lord's promise of peace and posterity, the two desires of this woman's heart. Little wonder her ache propelled her to touch the Lord's robe.

And it worked! At the instant she touched the fabric, she felt health rush through her body as she successfully stepped away—but she did not get away with her carefully worked out plan. The Messiah knew. He stopped and turned, asking, "Who touched my clothes?" (Mark 5:30). His gaze searched the crowd. She, shaken, I suspect, more by the miracle of health throbbing through her body than from fear of the Lord, confessed. Reassuring her, He said, "Daughter, thy faith hath made thee whole; go in peace, and be whole of thy plague" (Mark 5:34).

Three items of note come out of the Lord's actions. First, the Savior turned the spotlight, as it were, from Him to her. "Thy faith," He confirmed, with no mention of His Authority, allowed the miracle to happen. In this way He gave her confirmation, honor, and respect—things that she, as an adult, had never known.

Second, though the Lord shifted the spotlight, we cannot forget why the Lord knew He had been touched. According to the KJV, "Jesus, immediately knowing in himself that virtue had gone out of him, turned Him about" (Mark 5:30). "Virtue," the text says, "had gone out of him." What an unfortunate translation. It suggests she had somehow tainted Him, that this faith-filled woman had left Him impure, unholy. However, the word translated as "virtue" is actually "Power."[14] The Lord's healing Power flowed from Him to her, not her uncleanliness from her to Him. And His Power flowed not unconsciously or against His will, but according to it.

Third, we see His exquisite sympathy, so beautifully expressed in His first word to her, "Daughter."[15] At first the title seems strange, since she was a mature woman not much younger than Himself, but He did not address her as man to woman, but as Father to child.[16] Her faith had not only brought her physical wholeness, but also spiritual rebirth into the family of Christ. He had given her Power and she had become His daughter.

Here we see the interplay between faith, Authority, and Power. It was not the touch of the woman's hand, but her faith that secured the blessing. Even so, faith alone would not have worked. The Lord's Authority had to enter. She did not pull something from Him against His will; His superior sensitivity felt her faith and He decided to act, to use His Authority, in her favor. The reward was Power, an actual force, which flowed from Him to her, strengthening muscle, vein, and artery. Thus, she was physically made whole.

In fact, the Lord's Authority, drawing on the expiation He would make for her, did more. It took her case a step higher, to the realm of the spirit. There He used His Authority to judge her actions and reward her faith by making her a child of God. Of course, she still needed to complete specific tasks to make the blessings sure: baptism, covenant, and diligence; but her exquisite faith, which brought both miracles, was assurance that she would attend to these.

The Lord could, therefore, say, "go in peace" (Mark 5:34). Though it was the usual valediction of the time, the phrase meant more than freedom from fear of recrimination for having touched the Messiah, more than freedom from further physical pain and emotional distress. It connoted that dulcet calm and hope associated with knowing that she had been saved by God. Paul testified that this hope becomes "an anchor of the soul, both sure and stedfast" (Heb. 6:19). Joseph Smith expanded on the subject, saying, of the ancient Saints, that "having this promise sealed unto them, it was an anchor to the soul, sure and steadfast. Though the thunders might roll and lightnings flash, and earthquakes bellow, and war gather thick around, yet this hope and knowledge would support the soul in every hour of trial, trouble and tribulation."[17] Such hope brings real peace, in turn leading to real joy.

LOVE'S COST TO THE LORD

There are two more lessons to be learned before we press on. First, it cost the Lord something to heal. His Power went out of Him.

Consider Matthew's discourse when he testified that believers "brought unto him many that were possessed with devils: and he cast out the spirits with his word, and healed all that were sick: That it might be fulfilled which was spoken by Esaias the prophet, saying, Himself took our infirmities, and bare our sicknesses" (Matt. 8:16–17). When the Lord healed the woman, energy left Him and, for a moment, He felt her weakness, misery, and pain, and then He overcame it. As Paul testified, "Though he were a Son, yet learned he obedience by the things which he suffered" (Heb. 5:8).[18]

Second, and more importantly for our study, is that He took the grief, guilt, suffering, pain, and anguish of others—willingly. Isaiah said it best: "Surely he hath borne our griefs, and carried our sorrows . . . But He was wounded for our transgressions, he was bruised for our iniquities: the chastisement of our peace was upon him; and with his stripes we are healed" (Isa. 53:4–5).

It is amazing that He did it. What drove Him? Love—pure, sweet love. He did not have to suffer, He did not have to die for sin, but He did. He became a propitiation for our souls so that He might bring us, as He did the woman, rebirth, peace, and joy. With that, we come back to Lehi's vision of the tree and how the fruit brought him joy. That is the subject for the next chapter.

CHAPTER 5
THE PURE LOVE *of* CHRIST

The beauty of the tree which beckoned Lehi was the force within the pure love of Christ. His attraction revealed the almost irresistible, entirely desirable, nature of that power. Jeremiah knew of that irresistibility; he tried to resist. Being the Lord's emissary to a stiffnecked and hard-hearted people had brought him imprisonment, torture, and rejection. Finally, having had enough, Jeremiah decided to quit: "I said, I will not make mention of him, nor speak any more in his name. But his word was in mine heart as a burning fire shut up in my bones, and I was weary with forbearing, and I could not stay" (Jer. 20:9). The spirit of God, expressing His love, dwelt in Jeremiah's heart like fire in the bones, forcing him to continue to preach and warn. To those who obey, like Jeremiah, the Lord promised, "I will impart unto you of my Spirit, which shall enlighten your mind, which shall fill your soul with joy" (D&C 11:13).

Love is the vehicle by which God brings us to a fulness of joy. As King Benjamin knew, tasting of God's love causes us to have "exceedingly great joy" in our souls (Mosiah 4:11). How does love bring us to joy? To answer, we must understand what love is and how it works. Before we investigate, I need to make a point. We must not assume that our modern western definition of love fully conveys the scriptural meaning.[1] We use and misuse the word "love" so much that we are in danger of making the scriptures parrot our own ideas. We must let them speak for themselves and take our definition from them. Only then can we fully understand the word's depth, power, purpose, ability, and necessity in bringing us to joy.[2]

A SCRIPTURAL UNDERSTANDING OF LOVE

Of the many nouns that are associated with love, we will examine the four which have the greatest bearing on our understanding of love as it is used in the scriptures.[3] To remind us that I am defining these words a little differently than is usual in English, I will capitalize each one.

The first word we will explore is Affection.[4] The Apostle Paul condemned certain persons because they were, among other things, "without natural affection" (Rom. 1:31; 2 Tim. 3:3). The word he used denoted the feelings of one who was heartless, who had no Affection even for those whom a good person naturally loves.[5] Affection stands at the other end, defining that strong feeling that binds people into a defined group such as a club or fraternity.

However, its most pure and strong expression is found in the binding love of a family.[6] Indeed, its force promotes family love: Mom and Dad's love for their children and the children's love for their parents and one another. Paul's condemnation of those without "natural affection" shows us that Affection is a natural love that can arise easily and fully. However, it can also be destroyed when people become "lovers of their own selves, covetous, boasters, proud, blasphemers, disobedient to parents, unthankful, unholy" (2 Tim. 3:2). Affection is necessary to tame passion or erotic love, and places both in the service of God and family. Without it, these powers can become unbridled and hurtful. Affection promotes unselfishness, care, obedience, and safety. Therefore, its power safeguards and binds the family together by defining the correct relationship between its members—boundaries over which all refuse to step.

Children need a safe haven, a place to retreat from the fear and tension of a less than kind world. Affection assures that the home will be the place of security, protection, acceptance, and love. The word teaches us that family members, both parents and children, are meant to be friends—dear and best friends.

Righteousness promotes Affection and in so doing keeps the family—and society—strong and well protected. When society becomes unrighteous and selfish, Affection disappears and the family suffers. Therefore, the Savior prophesied that "because iniquity shall abound, the love of many shall wax cold" (JS–M 1:10, 30).[7] He understood that for many living in the last days, the home would cease to be a haven and become a hell. As a result, society would fail, family Affection having disappeared.[8]

The importance of Affection cannot be overstressed. The word connotes a necessary, relaxed love promoting happiness, unity, and tolerance. But therein we find a danger. Family members can become too relaxed around one another and demand too much acceptance. Some justify unwarranted acts because, at home, they can be themselves without having to put on any phony airs. They do not realize that we can become too comfortable and, thus, discourteous and even obnoxious toward those we are supposed to love the most. C. S. Lewis warns: "Affection is an affair of old clothes, and ease, of the unguarded moment, of liberties which would be ill-bred if we took them with strangers. But old clothes are one thing; to wear the same shirt till it stank would be another."[9] Affection does not uncouple love from respect and courtesy, especially at home. Affection never gives license to children for disrespect—thoughtlessness, negligence, rudeness, or abuse in any form. In truth, it is given to guard against them. Therefore, we should make every effort to promote it.[10]

I must note that the Gospel writers never used the word Affection to express the Father's love for His son.[11] The term they chose was "beloved."[12] This suggests that the early Christians assumed the importance and necessity of Affection but did not see in it that distinctive element of love with which the Father honored the Son and the Son the Father, nor that dimension of love which the gospel uniquely proclaimed.[13]

The next word we explore, which I will translate as Romance, does not bring us fully to a Christian understanding of love either. In fact, we find that, though the word was very popular in Greek literature, it never shows up in the New Testament.[14] So why should we even bother with it? For two reasons: first, its very absence lets us use it as a foil—meaning a revealing opposite—to more clearly see what the scriptures mean by love; and second, in our society, most people speak of love as defined by romance, that is, as romantic or sexual love. Even the Greeks used the word Romance to express a wide set of emotions ranging from a crude infatuation[15] to an exalted and pure passion.[16] No other word for love carried the breadth that Romance did.[17] What we must clarify is that Romance most often described a real, genuine love. It is a synonym for neither physical pleasure nor for lust, which can take place without love, as seen in prostitution or rape. Indeed, neither of these contain an ounce of Romance. But those feelings expressed in proper intimacy can only be described as Romance and, therefore, the physical dimension cannot be dissociated from it.[18]

Romance can be distinguished from other forms of love by two characteristics. First, it loves the worthy, meaning that the lover deems the object of love as worthy of it, whether it truly is or not. As the saying goes, beauty is in the eye of the beholder. Thus, there is a perceived attractiveness which draws the lover to the loved one. Others may not see it and openly say, "I just can't see what she/he sees in him/her." The point is that the lover sees in the other something of real worth or there would be no Romance.[19] The reason others do not see it is because they lack that dimension of love and, subsequently, sight or insight.

Second, the lover desires to possess the beloved. I have taught on the college level for over thirty years now, and I have yet to have a student say to me, "I'm absolutely head over heels in love with her, but I couldn't care less about who she marries." Once Romance strikes, lovers do all they can to woo, persuade, and possess.[20] Interestingly, on the positive side, it is Romance that guards against infidelity; on the negative, it can be the seedbed for jealousy. Of all the kinds of love, it is the most exclusive. It focuses on the loved one to such an extent that all other potential partners are seen as less worthy and, therefore, excluded from the circle of the beloved. It allows one to sacrifice all other such relationships for the sake of the one. Thus, Romance is the force behind monogamy and fidelity.

I hope I have explained the beauty, power, and importance of Romance well enough that you can sense that I am not talking about an inferior love that I am intending to contrast with a pure, "Christian" kind of love. We must recognize Romance as real and necessary in God's work, but it, like Affection, does not describe the special characteristics of God's love and the love the Savior commended. God's love, even for Israel, cannot be described in terms of Romance. The next word we study, Friendship, gets us closer.[21]

Friendship love, like romantic love, has a wide range of meanings. It often describes pure affection between persons of the same gender, but is not exclusive to that.[22] What we often do not realize is that it describes something that makes life gratifying and even rich. We could live in a world without friends, but our existence would be small and impoverished. It is true that modern man makes less of Friendship than his more ancient counterpart; Cicero wrote a book about its necessity and delight, while Aristotle classified Friendship as one of the cardinal virtues.[23] C. S. Lewis, in this light, noted it was "the least *natural* of loves; the least instinctive, organic biological, gregarious and necessary." He expounded his idea by saying that "without Eros [Romance] none of us would have been begotten and without Affection none of us would have been reared; but we can live and breed without Friendship. The species, biologically considered, has no need of it." Going on, he says, "Friendship is unnecessary, like philosophy, like art. . . . It has no survival value; rather it is one of those things which give value to survival."[24]

Friendship is built on something that friends have in common, like taste, interest, or bias, but which others do not share. While Romance is a private love between two people, Friendship is broader, though not a complete public love. Still, it can exist between quite a number of people. It spawns no jealousy. It may begin with simple interest but, developed over time, it can turn into esteem so great that often "each member of the circle feels, in his secret heart, humbled before all the rest. Sometimes he wonders what he is doing there among his betters."[25]

The great benefit of Friendship is that it brings out the best in each participant. Each member finds strength in and reinforcement from the others. However, there is also a downside. Lewis notes that "friendship (as the ancients saw) can be a school of virtue; but also (as they did not see) a school of vice. It is ambivalent. It makes good men better and bad men worse."[26] As the social circle can strengthen virtues, it can reinforce vices. The group can rationalize a stand to the point that it refuses to accept any law or rule except that which is within the association, because that is what defines the self-identity of the circle of friends.[27] Thus, it can become a hothouse in which narrow-mindedness, intolerance, bigotry, and lawlessness flourish. This can grow into pride with its extreme exclusiveness forbidding entrance to all outsiders with a fierceness and absoluteness beyond that of any scribbled "No Girls Allowed" sign.

However, the scriptures do not view the word Friendship in any negative way. Indeed, John used the verb form to describe the relationship between the Father and the Son, saying, "the Father loveth the Son, and sheweth him all things that himself doeth" (John 5:20).[28] He further has the Savior use it to describe the Father's feelings for all the disciples and the disciples' feelings for the Savior: "The Father himself loveth [feels friendship toward] you, because ye have loved [felt friendship toward] me, and have believed that I came out from God" (John 16:27). In this regard, the Savior said to His disciples, "I call you not servants; for the servant knoweth not what his lord doeth: but I have called you friends [confidants[29]]; for all things that I have heard of my Father I have made known unto you" (John 15:15). Friendship, especially that contained within the family, gets us close to the scriptural sense of love, but we are not quite there.[30] This brings us to the last word in our study.

Of the choices available in the very rich Greek language for love, the New Testament prefers one noun above all others to express its particular view. That word is often translated as Charity.[31] What is of note is that the Greek noun was rarely used in pre-Biblical Greek literature before the Christians adopted it.[32] The Septuagint, the Old Testament translated into Greek some time between the third and first centuries B.C., uses the word twenty times, showing that it had some use in Jewish circles and, therefore, would have been known to the early Jewish Christians through that source. Still, its use, even among the Jews, was rare.[33] The reason the early Christians may have chosen this relatively obscure word to express their idea about love was because its very scarcity allowed them to put their own spin on it.[34] In other words, it did not come with a lot of semantic baggage. Indeed, the force of the word was rather insipid and weak before the Saints took it as their own and breathed a pure and powerful fire into it.[35]

THE NEW TESTAMENT MEANING OF LOVE

So what did the early Christians want to tell the world about love as revealed by Jesus? A good place to start is by contrasting Charity with Romance. Unlike the latter, Charity seeks neither the love of the worthy nor its possession. The word expresses a love freely given without respect of worth or merit. Romance is ignited through the apparent attractiveness of the loved one, whereas Charity loves even those who would be otherwise unappealing, even repulsive. Its reach is very broad. Not only does it include those who have nothing to give in return, but also those who would spurn and abuse it.[36]

It is this spin, given by the early Church, which allowed Charity to describe exactly their new understanding of God's love, a love through which He extended His grace to old and new Israel.[37] Beyond that, God's love spread even further, to that portion of the world which did not even know Him and worshiped in His place dumb idols of gold, silver, wood, and stone. As noted, He gave His Son to a world that was anything but worthy of Him. I cannot help but think of God's statement to Enoch, "I can stretch forth mine hands and hold all the creations which I have made; and mine eye can pierce them also, and among all the workmanship of mine hands there has not been so great wickedness as among thy brethren" (Moses 7:36). Please note, however, that wickedness did not repulse God's love; instead this unworthiness caused it to act in greater abundance, causing Him, as it were, to send His Son. In the same way, the Charity of the Son caused Him, as it were, to pay the debt, suffering death and hell even for this wicked, cruel, and hurtful world.

OUR NEED FOR THE SAVIOR

The whole thrust of the early Apostles' use of the word Charity underscores how desperately we need God's Son. The central idea in their testimony is that because of love, God sent His only begotten Son to a world that was in so much trouble that no one less could save it. And the Son did not demur, insisting that "they that are whole have no need of the physician, but they that are sick: I came not to call the righteous, but sinners to repentance" (Mark 2:17). What He was polite enough not to say was that everyone is sick. I fear that the Lord's statement may not appear as shocking and revolutionary as it was to those who first heard it. The Jews insisted that God loved the righteous but abhorred the sinner, and would have nothing to do with him. The Lord's statement was nothing short of a frontal attack on their outlook, and He could hardly have expressed it more strongly.[38]

In this regard, notice that Jesus used the word "came" in describing His mission; He "came" to heal sinners.[39] That one word identifies His charge as outlined by God—to heal sinners. Simple as it seems, that was God's full intent in sending the Son. Thus, Charity expressed the positive predisposition and spontaneous love God had and has for sinful man. Further, because of this He continually pours out this love in spite of humankind's most stubborn misbehavior toward one another and Him.[40] "For God sent not his Son into the world to condemn the world; but that the world through him might be saved" (John 3:17).

Allow me to provide one example of Christ's charity. The Savior was teaching one day, early in His ministry, to a packed house. Friends of a man stricken with paralysis had deep faith in the Lord's ability to heal. They, therefore, carried their friend on a litter to see Him. When they could find no way in, they took the paralyzed man, via outside stairs, to the roof, and, breaking out a section of the awning, lowered him into the courtyard before the Lord.[41] Seeing their faith, the Lord said to the man, "Son, thy sins be forgiven thee" (Mark 2:5). This produced quite a shock among the Pharisees and scribes scattered among His audience and they asked one another, "Why doth this man thus speak blasphemies? who can forgive sins but God only?" (Mark 2:7).

The untold tale in Mark's narrative, and where the bite lies, was the belief by many Jews that long-term illness was caused by sin. This meant that the truly pious (in their own eyes) should have nothing to do with the sick. Thus, they would have left the paralytic strapped to his bed—or, for that matter, the leper to his pain—but Jesus would do neither. He readily forgave the man, taking upon Himself the pain of that sin-filled soul.

Charity allowed Jesus to reach out even to His critics and try to bring them into the circle of His love. So He asked: "Whether is it easier to say to the sick of the palsy, Thy sins be forgiven thee; or to say, Arise, and take up thy bed, and walk? But that ye may know that the Son of man hath power on earth to forgive sins, (he saith to the sick of the palsy,) I say unto thee, Arise, and take up thy bed, and go thy way into thine house" (Mark 2:9–11), which the man promptly did, to the astonishment and wonder of all. Those present should have understood the inclusive nature of the Lord's kind of love for both saint and sinner.

All the teachings and practice of the early Church indicate a complete reversal in ideas concerning the values of the natural man. Note Jesus' emphasis that His disciples should not love as the world does—not even when it loves at its best and purest. He taught that we should love as God does, He who "maketh His sun to rise on the evil and on the good, and sendeth rain on the just and on the unjust. For if ye love them which love you, what reward have ye? do not even the publicans the same? And if ye salute your brethren only, what do ye more than others? do not even the publicans so? Be ye therefore perfect, even as your Father which is in heaven is perfect" (Matt. 5:45–48). Note that His admonition is to love everyone, because that is how God loves. His love bypasses neither the ungrateful nor the disagreeable. God's love is not conditioned by acceptance, righteousness, or kindness. He simply loves us because we are.

Note that this is the context of the Savior's admonition to be perfect. It was the apostle John who taught that "God is love; and he that dwelleth in love dwelleth in God," and through this we become perfect "because as he [God] is, so are we in this world" (1 Jn 4:16–17). As the Father's perfect love reaches out to include all in the bounds of His goodwill and service, so should our own. How else could we be "perfect" like our Heavenly Father?[42]

THREE PARABLES OF THE LORD

The Savior illustrated the point with His now famous parable of the prodigal son. As Jesus tells the story, the son was truly profligate. He went far from home so he could do with his inheritance as he pleased with no disapproving eyes. He spent his fortune in riotous living and he spent it all. Nothing was left. Afterward, so extreme was his want that he, a Jew, not only hired himself out to a Gentile, but also as a swineherd. His want was so great that he was even tempted to eat the pigs' food. He had no money, no merit, no self-respect—

nothing. He decided to go home, knowing he had not a single claim to anything. He fully understood that by his own choice he had forfeited all. So he determined, "I will arise and go to my father, and will say unto him, Father, I have sinned against heaven, and before thee, And am no more worthy to be called thy son: make me as one of thy hired servants" (Luke 15:18–19). He could not have been more right, for he deserved no more.

In spite of his actions, however, he was welcomed back not only with the open arms of a loving father but also with the music of joy and a feast of the fatted calf. Nor did he become a servant in his father's house, but the beloved and newly reborn son of a righteous father.

Many of us can identify with the older brother, who refused to be part of such seeming injustice. His father's request that he come and join the fun did not move him, nor did his father's assurance, "Son, thou art ever with me, and all that I have is thine" (Luke 15:31).

The older brother suffered from his own problem, a lack of love, and it not only blinded him to the joy of the moment but also to something more important. He had ever been with his father. For all the years his younger brother had lost the association, the older brother had retained it. Yet, he never saw this as a blessing. His was not a life of joy with his father, but a life of drudgery on the farm. Because of his outlook, he never realized what a blessing it had been to work, and sweat, and succeed with his father. His eyes were only on the end time when the farm would be his alone.

The Savior's story, of course, underscores Heavenly Father's unbounded love, the affection that causes Him such joy when sinners repent and come home. So what if they have nothing to give? That does not matter to God. He demands no minimum fee, no down payment before he will accept them—only that they return. As Paul testified, "By the righteousness of one the free gift came upon all men unto justification of life" (Rom. 5:18). And Lehi rejoiced that "the way is prepared from the fall of man, and salvation is free" (2 Ne. 2:4). God demands no payment for giving His love nor its benefits in the Atonement of His Son, but we must come home if we are going to feel it. Redemption does not come to those who choose to associate with swine over fathers, even if they are the pigs' herders.

In this light, consider the point the Savior made in another parable. As He tells it, a certain lord hired servants to assist him harvest his grapes. These he hired early in the morning, promising to pay them a "penny"[43] (as translated in the King James Version), the usual wage for a day's work. They readily agreed and the work commenced. Seeing the harvest needed more assistance, the lord hired additional helpers throughout the day, telling them he would be fair with the wage if they would come to work immediately. He hired the last group just an hour before sundown. With the help of these he was able to finish the job. What happened many find both surprising and disquieting:

> The lord of the vineyard saith unto his steward, Call the labourers, and give them their hire, beginning from the last unto the first. And when they came that were hired about the eleventh hour, they received every man a penny. But when the first came, they supposed that they should have received more; and they likewise received every man a penny. And when they had received it, they murmured against the goodman of the house, Saying, These last have wrought but one hour, and thou hast made them equal unto us, which have borne the burden and heat of the day. But he answered one of them, and said, Friend, I do thee no wrong: didst not thou agree with me for a penny? Take that thine is, and go thy way: I will give unto this last, even as unto thee. Is it not lawful for me to do what I will with mine own? Is thine eye evil, because I am good? So the last shall be first, and the first last: for many be called, but few chosen (Matt. 20:8–16).

How does this story strike you? My students feel the lord of the vineyard really was quite unfair and wonder at the Savior's point. Let's explore the meaning by contrasting His parable with one popular among the rabbis not long after the Savior's time. According to this account:

> [A] king . . . hired many labourers, one of whom so distinguished himself by industry and skill that the king took

him by the hand and walked up and down with him. In the evening the labourers came, and the skillful one among them, to receive their pay. The king gave them all the same pay. Wherefore those who had worked the whole day murmured, and spake: We have worked the whole day, and this man only two hours, and yet he also has received his whole pay.[44]

Note the similarity between the two parables. Both focus on laborers who work vastly different amounts of time for the same wage. In both, the laborers who worked the longest complain of the unfairness of the situation. What is different between the two parables is the moral. According to the rabbis, the king replied, "This man hath wrought more in two hours than you in the whole day."[45]

The rabbis resolve the tension by doing what is instinctive to the natural man—they appeal to merit. Thus, all were justly rewarded because the pay was for work accomplished, not for hours put in on the job. Jesus' point stands in marked contrast to their view. The last laborers in His parable did one twelfth the work but received the whole wage, and that *is* His point. It underscores the fallacy underlying the popular saying that "if you are good, you will go to heaven." The idea behind that statement is that it is totally possible for us to be so good that we can earn our way to heaven. It insists that we will be justly rewarded for all our hard work. The fallacy is twofold: first, it implies righteousness in exchange for profit; second, it suggests that we really can be good (read perfect) enough to earn our way into heaven.

The Lord's parable speaks against this view. Had the Savior wanted to, He could have had the lord of the vineyard give each laborer exactly his due. You see, there was a twelfth part of a "penny." The coin was called a *pondion*.[46] However, fairness was not the Lord's point. The parable insists that God's love cannot be divided into portions. In reality, God does not deal with any of us fairly—if He did, we would all suffer spiritual and eternal death. Paul said it best: "All have sinned, and come short of the glory of God" (Rom. 3:23).

Fortunately, God deals with us not on the basis of merit, but on that of grace. We must see salvation for what it is: the active response to the call, when it is extended, to become the chosen and to work diligently today—not for reward, not to earn a way into God's favor or into His heaven, but to accomplish the work with the same kind of love that called us to serve.[47]

I fear, too, that we miss the point of another parable, that of the publican and the Pharisee. According to the Lord, "Two men went up into the temple to pray; the one a Pharisee, and the other a publican. The Pharisee stood and prayed thus with himself, God, I thank thee, that I am not as other men are, extortioners, unjust, adulterers, or even as this publican. I fast twice in the week, I give tithes of all that I possess" (Luke 18:10–12). We are too ready to castigate his act, and it is little wonder, for his prayer quite naturally repulses us. We dismiss his prayer as being a gross exaggeration. But it was not, and this is where the sting of the parable lies. He truly was expressing reality. His prayer was certainly in bad taste, and he can be chastened for that, but not for any lack of veracity. He was not like other men, and his fasting and offerings, freely and fully given, prove the point. He really was not an adulterer or an extortioner. His problem was not with the distance he had traveled on the road; he had gone a long way. The problem was that he was on the wrong road, one of his own making instead of God's. He expected to win heaven through his own merit, with little or no help from the Father. The publican, with the heartfelt confession, said simply, "God be merciful to me a sinner," threw himself on God's grace, and, according to the Lord, "went down to his house justified rather than the other: for every one that exalteth himself shall be abased; and he that humbleth himself shall be exalted" (Luke 18:13–14).[48]

Do not, however, jump to the wrong conclusion. God's love is not, as is so often expressed, unconditional. The fact that He loves us does not mean that we can get away with sin. In fact, it assures us that we won't. That discussion, however, will have to wait for chapter six.

A MODERN PARABLE

For now, let me summarize by sharing with you a modern parable.[49] According to this story, there were two brothers. The younger, Ralph, remained ever active in the Church while the elder,

George, ran away at a young age and lived a hard life, even losing his Church membership. Some forty years later, missionaries ran into George. He invited them in and listened—really listened—to what they had to say. He was touched and decided to repent and come back into the fold. Working with his bishop, he put his past behind him and prepared for baptism. When his bishop asked him who he would like to perform the ordinance, he requested his brother Ralph. George's bishop consulted Ralph's bishop in order to make preparations.

Ralph's bishop invited Ralph into his office to give him the good news. If he expected Ralph to be thrilled, he was unpleasantly mistaken. Ralph became angry and refused to take any part. He told the bishop of the heartache George had caused his parents, and detailed the sins of which George was guilty. Now, he said, George wanted to come back as though nothing had happened, to get back into the fold in full fellowship after all the hurt he caused, to receive the same reward with those who had worked their whole lives in service. No, Ralph assured the bishop, he would have nothing to do with such unfairness.

The bishop paused for a moment, and then, under that inspiration which comes with the keys of discernment, said: "Ralph, sin lies at the door, and you had better repent or you will, in the end, lose all. You have two problems. The first is envy. There was desire in you, at times, to do what George was doing. That is the reason you kept track of every misdeed, all the while feeling resentment that you could not do it too, but you lacked the audacity to rebel from your parents' wishes. The second is closely related. You never really found joy in the Church. Service has been like a ball and chain from which you could neither free yourself nor get any comfort. Because you never recognized or cherished the blessings and joys of giving, you cannot see all that your brother has missed by being out of the kingdom for so long."

This parable gives us a kind of gauge by which we can assess our own attitude. Do we feel a little sorrow for those who begin work in the vineyard late in the day because they will not have a chance to experience the joy of long service and extended association with the lord of the vineyard? Those who do not fully love the Father or His work, who do not see associating with Him, working with Him, even aching with Him, as joy, can never count the moments as privilege or feel genuine sorrow for those who missed spending time with Him. The converted rejoice in the knowledge that those who come to the vineyard, even late in the day, will not be one whit behind them! The point is, we will get our penny and they will get the same. God is the good lord of the vineyard and takes care of all His workers, doing not what is strictly fair in our view, but what is right.

THE TREE OF LOVE

Lehi knew the joy of the work and understood its source, the love of God, symbolized in the beautiful tree. Nephi added another dimension. To his brothers, he explained that the tree "was a representation of the tree of life" (1 Ne. 15:22). The idea harkens back to Eden, where that tree had a property such that one could "eat, and live for ever" (Gen. 3:22). It came to symbolize eternal life. As the Lord told John, "To him that overcometh will I give to eat of the tree of life, which is in the midst of the paradise of God" (Rev. 2:7). Nephi shows us that the imagery of the tree links love and eternal life, the prerequisites of a fulness of joy.

Nephi testified that God's love "sheddeth itself abroad in the hearts of the children of men; wherefore, it is the most desirable above all things" (1 Ne. 11:22). The context points to the Savior, God's love-gift to humankind, and includes His birth, ministry, Atonement, and Resurrection. Out of these comes salvation to most of humankind and exaltation for the faithful. This is, as the angel said to Nephi, "most joyous to the soul" (v. 23). Once we see, desire, and receive the salvation promised by and through the Savior, it brings us a fulness of joy.

So if that is the case, what did the fruit of the tree represent? Remember, it was partaking of that fruit, not the mere sight of the beautiful tree, that filled Lehi "with exceedingly great joy," and by which he knew it was "desirable above all other fruit" (1 Ne. 8:12). An explanation of the fruit is in the next chapter. Here, allow me to pull together the ideas found in this and chapter four by relating an experience.

THE POWER OF CHRIST

While I was teaching Institute, a woman came to see me. An easterner, a mother of two, a divorcee, and a fairly recent convert, she had moved west to be near the Church. She was back in school trying to develop skills which would secure her a good job. She was struggling to find her place in a church that seemed male dominated.

As we talked, she displayed both frustration and resentment. I became concerned and shared my fear that her vexation could drive her from the Church. That made her pause. She then assured me that such would not be the case. She explained that it was her way to overstate a position, then push it, to make others better defend their own. The problem was, she admitted, that it often made her appear to care more about a matter than she really did. She then shared with me her love for the Church and why it meant so much to her.

She was the product of a very abusive home, her father forcing her into immoral activities. In defense, she learned to lie. It did not work all the time, but often enough to be useful. Once she freed herself from that environment, however, she tried to stop lying and found she could not. She told me how she fought it, but never won. She explained how she had found a fine man and how they grew in love. He was willing to accept her and her vice on condition that she would not lie to him. She promised him she would not. They married and, though she tried to fight the lie, she continued to use it, even with him. She told me how she could see what the lie was doing to him and her marriage, how desperately she hated it, how hard she tried to stop it, and how she failed. Finally, her lies killed his love and their marriage.

Not long after the divorce, she said, two young women came to her door offering peace and prayer. She allowed them in and found out they were Mormon missionaries. She listened to their message, felt the peace of their prayer, and invited them back. She took the discussions, read the Book of Mormon, and believed. She even began attending the Church, living the Word of Wisdom, and praying. She also continued to lie. Still, she wanted her children to have what she could not, and asked the missionaries to arrange for their baptism.

When the missionaries invited her to be baptized, she refused, making up an excuse. In other words, she told me, she lied—even to them. And that was the reason she knew she could never be baptized.

She could not repent. She was a liar and there was nothing she could do about it, except face the awful doom pronounced in the Book of Mormon, for the liar "shall be thrust down to hell" (2 Ne. 9:34).

Shortly before the children's baptism, she was interviewed by the branch president. He wanted to know why the Church was good enough for her children and not for her. She told him her lie, but he would not buy it and pressed for more. Finally, with bitter tears, she told him her story. His response shook her. He challenged her to be baptized, saying he felt very impressed that if she would act in faith, the Lord would come into her life and help her do what she could not do alone. She told me how she agonized over the decision, but finally, knowing the gospel was true and hoping the Lord would assist her, she consented.

One of the elders she had come to know confirmed her. The Spirit spoke through him and promised her that God knew her faith and courage, and He would reward her. She told me that a spirit of peace settled upon her and she felt a strength she had never experienced before. That, she said, had happened three years ago. From that time to this, she assured me, she had never lied.

Unlike the woman with the issue of blood, my friend's malady was not physical, but spiritual. Yet, like the other woman, she reached out to Christ in faith and was healed. She entered into a newness of life. Her rebirth did not come, as John stated, due to her will, desire, or passion. She had tried those and failed. It took her faith and the Lord's power to do it.

She knew, as John had testified, that when one is born of God, he cannot continue in sin because the Spirit of God is there to assist. (See JST, 1 Jn. 3:9.) Let us not forget, however, that the Spirit came through the Lord's Authority. He judged her case as He had the woman with the issue of blood, and found her faith sufficient. He gave her Power to overcome and then acted as her propitiator, reconciling her to God and to the Spirit.

As for the missionaries and an inspired branch president, they rejoiced in her baptism and her cleansing. There was no resentment that she had entered the field of labor later in the day. They rejoiced that she, too, received her penny and would not be one whit behind them. They all, as it were, enjoyed the feast of the fatted calf as one.

I have one last point. Usually, the Lord demands that one cease sinning before baptism. For reasons I do not fully understand, He insisted she be baptized first. I am impressed that her deep and abiding sin did not repulse Him. Rather, His Charity took her in. I think He judged her case and determined that she needed the gift of the Holy Ghost as a constant source of Power. She had already shown good faith in living much of the gospel and was determined to do more. I wonder, too, if it was not her own love that played a part—that determination to give her sons what she felt she could never have. It was that love that brought her to the interview and to eventual confession. It was her Affection that brought her to Charity and then into joy.

As I said earlier, love is the vehicle by which God brings us to joy. How? Love provides the drive to respond to God's call and become the chosen. It gives the fervor to work diligently, not for reward or favor, but for the good of others. In that loving selflessness comes eternal glory and a fulness of joy.

CHAPTER 6
LOVE *and* CALLING *and* ELECTION

In Lehi's vision, he partook of the fruit of the tree that represented love, and it filled his soul with joy. If the tree symbolically blended the aspects of eternal life and pure love, what did the fruit represent? Let us begin our exploration by turning to the writings of Peter, he who, according to Joseph Smith, "penned the most sublime language of any of the apostles."[1]

INSIGHTS FROM PETER'S SECOND EPISTLE

Peter wrote his epistles just at the twilight of his dispensation. The dark period of apostasy was beginning to take hold of the Church of Jesus Christ. He wrote with urgency, knowing that his death was imminent and that perverse forces were already at work pulling the Saints away from the truth that God had revealed through His Son. We can imagine Peter's concern for the faithful Saints, knowing that soon all priesthood authority would be taken from the earth. In his epistles, we see his earnest desire to protect them, making certain that they secured their just reward before the apostasy came and God's power was taken from the earth.

With that urgency, Peter testified to the Saints "that shortly I must put off this my tabernacle, even as our Lord Jesus Christ hath shewed me" (2 Pet. 1:14).[2] Knowing that his death was imminent, he explained, "I think it meet, as long as I am in this tabernacle, to stir you up by putting you in remembrance" of what they could achieve (2 Pet. 1:13). The Greek words translated as "to stir up" mean "to arouse," "to motivate," or "to prompt to action."[3] Peter wanted to motivate the Saints to achieve a specific goal. He admonished them to "make your calling and election sure," and in so doing, "ye shall never fall" (2 Pet. 1:10). Indeed, "an entrance shall be ministered unto you abundantly into the everlasting kingdom of our Lord and Savior Jesus Christ" (2 Pet. 1:11). In spite of the seductive forces pulling the Church into apostasy, Peter knew there was a way to make sure the faithful Saints would not lose their exaltation. It entailed making their calling and election sure.

THE MEANING OF MAKING A CALLING AND ELECTION SURE

Defining the terms he used will greatly assist us in understanding his message. The word translated "calling" means "to be invited."[4] The Greek term denoted an invitation extended for a specific event at a certain time. The invitation could be for activities as diverse as entertainment or work. Those who accepted the invitation, showing up and doing what was expected, enjoyed the reward of their effort. Each person invited was free to accept or reject the call, but rejection forfeited any reward. In theological terms, we accept the Lord's call by responding to the invitation to have faith in Him, entering into His covenant, and striving to keep His commandments. As we do so, we secure for ourselves the promised reward of eternal life. In other words, our continued faithfulness guarantees that we will receive the reward, and thus it is "made sure."[5]

In the early Christian context, as in the Church today, God calls us to the gospel covenant. He invites us to be born again and receive the promise of eternal life, on the conditions of obedience and service. This call stems from our preexistent faithfulness and the foreordination we received under God's hand.[6] Thus, the call came because of worthiness in premortality and faithfulness here (see Alma 13:3–5). A person could be foreordained but, due to faithlessness in mortality, be unworthy of the call. It is for this reason that Paul prayed that the Thessalonian Saints would remain worthy of the invitation (2 Thes. 1:11); he feared their loss of faith, despite his knowledge of their foreordination.

Closely associated with calling is election. The word Peter uses means "to select, choose, or pick out," and implies selection because of superb quality.[7] The word can also be translated "chosen." Therefore, the elect and the chosen are one and the same. The use of the term in the scriptures presupposes that a call has been both extended and accepted. Once God issues the call, the divine will acts to select and direct the worthy person to positions in which he may accomplish the preappointed tasks outlined in the invitation. A person becomes the elect of God by accepting and fulfilling the call. The Doctrine and Covenants states: "Mine elect hear my voice and harden not their hearts" (D&C 29:7). The elect are that subset of the called who actually accept the invitation and then respond with full purpose of heart.[8] Fulfilling the call assures them of the reward. In this way, they make the promised reward for their election sure.[9]

Sadly, the scriptures point out that many are called to the service but few become elect because "their hearts are set so much upon the things of this world, and [they] aspire to the honors of men" (D&C 121:35). Thus, they forfeit their reward.

PAUL'S OUTLINE OF THE PLAN OF SALVATION

Those whose faithful response to the work makes them the elect, are beloved of God (see Col. 3:12). Through their service, they, in turn, grow in their love toward Him. Paul understood the results. "And we know," he taught, "that all things work together for good to them that love God, to them who are the called according to his purpose" (Rom. 8:28). Because the saint loves God, he fulfills the call, thereby allowing God's choicest blessings to flow eternally unto him. Paul taught further that those "whom he [God] did foreknow, he also did predestinate to be conformed to the image of his Son, that he might be the firstborn among many brethren. Moreover whom he did predestinate, them he also called: and whom he called, them he also justified: and whom he justified, them he also glorified" (Rom. 8:29–30).

Paul here outlines very briefly the plan of salvation as he sees it. In simple terms, it begins with God's foreknowledge of His spirit children. God predestined, or foreordained, certain children to accomplish specific tasks in mortality based on their righteousness in the premortal world.[10] The Father then predetermined that those who fulfilled their tasks would become like the Savior—children of God and heirs of glory. While here in mortality, those who were foreordained receive the call to service. Those who respond—the elect—are forgiven of their sins by God. That is, He justifies them. Those whom He justifies then receive glory or eternal life in the world to come.

In order to assure the elect's success in the endeavor, God gave His Son to redeem them from death and hell. That the Father was willing to pay such a high ransom suggests the value He places on the elect. It reveals the degree to which He is willing to work with, forgive, and justify all His children. The Savior's love compounds the Father's; therefore, the chosen have the love of both Christ and the Father acting in their behalf. Nothing can separate them from that love. In all things, testified Paul, "we are more than conquerors through him that loved us. For I am persuaded, that neither death, nor life, nor angels, nor principalities, nor powers, nor things present, nor things to come, Nor height, nor depth, nor any other creature, shall be able to separate us from the love of God, which is in Christ Jesus our Lord" (Rom. 8:37–39). All this love assists the elect in making their calling and election sure, or, in other words, receiving eternal glory.

Peter outlined in careful detail what the Saints had do to make their calling and election sure. Before studying what he had to say, I need to make a point. What 2 Peter teaches about making one's calling and election sure only hints at what the prophet had in mind[11]. Insights given through Joseph Smith help us more fully round out Peter's intent. We will first look at what 2 Peter teaches in its biblical context and then at the additional insights given through the Restoration.

THE IMPORTANCE of KNOWING GOD

Peter clearly enunciated what is necessary to make our calling and election sure. He revealed the foundation of the whole process in his invocation: "grace and peace be multiplied unto you through the knowledge of God, and of Jesus our Lord, According as his divine power hath given unto us all things that pertain unto life and godliness, through the knowledge of him that hath called us to glory and virtue" (2 Pet. 1:2–3). There are four items we need to pay attention to in Peter's salutation.

First, the word translated in English as "knowledge" does not convey the force of the Greek word Peter chose. The Greeks have two related words that are translated as the English word "knowledge."[12] The first means knowledge gained by learning and acquiring skills, and the second, the one Peter used, means to know fully or completely. Such knowledge is acquired through experience with the person, place, or thing known.[13] In spiritual terms we can think of this fulness of knowledge as a sure testimony of God and His Son revealed through the unmistakable power of the Holy Ghost. Joseph Smith taught that "the principle of knowledge is the principle of salvation," and that "the principle of salvation is given us through the knowledge of Jesus Christ."[14]

Second, out of knowing God, that is, having a sure testimony, comes grace and peace. Here the word "grace" can best be understood in terms discussed in a previous chapter: power to overcome the natural man and be born again. In spiritual terms, peace denotes that feeling of assurance we have when we know we have a loving relationship with the Father.[15]

Third, God has extended a call to the Christians. The call is not solely the work of His ministry. Rather it invites them into an ever-growing association with the Father and the Son, which will naturally include the work of His ministry.

Finally, Peter looks to the ultimate purpose of the call, that of "glory and virtue." Again, the English words can benefit from a better understanding of Greek definitions. "Glory" is associated with radiance, splendor, effulgence and, in the biblical context, the very presence of God. It is a visual manifestation of His Holy Spirit. Glory is part of God's nature, and it centers in Him. It extends from Him to fill the immensity of space, and, though not unfelt, it is unseen unless He determines otherwise (see D&C 88:5–13, 40–41, 67–68).

Because God controls this power, He can extend it to dwell in greater fullness in His children. The book of Exodus supplies a somewhat humorous example. Moses, atop Sinai for the second time in only a few days, basked in the presence and glory of the Lord. For nearly six weeks he received divine instruction under that power. During that time, the Lord wrote His revelation to Israel on tablets of stone. When completed, Moses brought the written commandments to the camp of Israel. To his surprise, no one received him. In fact, with fear obviously gripping them, they retreated. Moses was momentarily perplexed at their reaction because he "wist not that the skin of his face shone." The prophet had to persuade Aaron and other leaders to approach him so he could instruct them (see Ex. 34:28–35).

Only when the congregation saw that these men were able to stand before Moses without harm did they come back and in turn receive instruction. However, the people must have felt quite uncomfortable in the glory radiating from Moses because he had to place a thick veil over his face before instructing them. For several days, until the radiance subsided, he had to wear the veil in his general dealings with the people, "but when Moses went in before the Lord [into the tabernacle] to speak with him, he took the vail off, until he came out" (Exodus 34:34). Until the radiance finally dimmed, Moses had to keep veiling and unveiling his face.

But why did glory trouble the children of Israel? It was because Moses was manifesting the purity, power, and intellect of Jehovah which Israel was unable to abide, albeit in a diminutive and reflected state. They were too spiritually immature. Their souls, as yet unholy, felt discomfort in the mere echoes of the divine intelligence that still dwelt in Moses.

From the Doctrine and Covenants we learn that "the glory of God is intelligence, or, in other words, light and truth" (D&C 93:36). Light, as used in this scriptural context, means capacitating power. Its touch enables us to do things not otherwise possible, such as perform miracles or understand the mysteries of godliness.[16] Truth, again in its scriptural context, is knowledge of existence.[17] God's intelligence consists in His capacity or power (light) to know all existence and, thereby, understand all truth.[18] The power associated with this ability looks to humans like scintillating light, sometimes described as "cloven tongues like as of fire" (Acts 2:1–4). Moses, partaking of the glory of God, was able to understand the things of God and communicate them to the children of Israel.

But there is another aspect of glory we must not overlook. John testified that "God is light" (1 Jn. 1:5), and that "God is love" (1 Jn. 4:16). Is there a connection between light and love? It appears there is. Those who experience the glory of the Lord note the incredible love associated with it. One person believed that God's fire can "best be described as personified love." Another called it "unconditional love" with the power to touch, lift, and transform. Having studied the phenomenon, Professor Brent Top concluded that "in some inexplicable way, this light is also love; the light being the source of everything good in the world and in the eternities."[19]

Now, Peter says that God has called the Saints to partake of this love-power coupled with the understanding of truth it brings. Further, Peter says that God has called us to "virtue." The force of the Greek term emphasizes God's moral excellence, expressed through divine service. Peter's thought, to retranslate the Greek text, is that God has "formally invited us to share in his own glory and moral excellence" through acceptance of the call.[20] Note that God is calling us to become as He is: we are to partake of *His* glory and *His* virtue.

Though he does not enumerate them, Peter goes on to say that, through the power of God, there are "given unto us exceeding great and precious promises" (2 Pet. 1:4). If we study the scriptures, however, it is not hard to find out what these promises are. For example, as part of His instructions to the Twelve just before His ascension, the Lord commanded the Apostles not to leave Jerusalem, "but wait for the promise of the Father, which, saith He, ye have heard of me. For John truly baptized with water; but ye shall be baptized with the Holy Ghost not many days hence" (Acts 1:4–5). That promise was fulfilled on the day of Pentecost. The power, descending like fire, enabled the Apostles to speak in tongues. Peter explained to a fascinated crowd that what they were experiencing was caused by the power of the resurrected Savior: "Therefore being by the right hand of God exalted, and having received of the Father the promise of the Holy Ghost, he hath shed forth this, which ye now see and hear" (Acts 2:33). When his hearers determined to join the Church, Peter declared that "ye shall receive the gift of the Holy Ghost. For the promise is unto you, and to your children, and to all that are afar off, even as many as the Lord our God shall call" (Acts 2:38–39).

The scriptures give deeper understanding to Peter's words. Those who separate themselves from the world, becoming holy, also become the children of God and inherit eternal life (see 2 Cor. 6:18). We also see this teaching in the words of the Savior just before His death. He promised His disciples that, if they would love Him and keep His commandments, He would send them another comforter, "even the Spirit of truth" (John 14:16–17; see also 16:7–15). Paul called this spirit the "holy Spirit of promise" (Eph. 1:13). According to the Doctrine and Covenants, "This Comforter is the promise which I give unto you of eternal life, even the glory of the celestial kingdom; Which glory is that of the church of the Firstborn, even of God, the holiest of all, through Jesus Christ his Son" (D&C 88:4–5).

We shall learn more about the Holy Spirit of Promise below; for now it is important to note what activates this power. Peter is clear on the subject. He says that the key is "full knowledge," or in other words, sure testimony.[21] Thus we can infer that those who pay the price to get the testimony receive the Lord's personal promise that they shall have eternal life. Peter says that in this way we may escape the corruption in the world—created by misspent passion—and actually become partakers of the divine nature.

Peter well understood that the power of God, granted to the faithful, was the key to escaping the seductive forces in the world and the false teachers within the Church. Knowing God fully[22] unlocks this power and makes it active. So Peter outlines in 2 Peter 1:5–8 the way for Christians to gain sure knowledge, with its accompanying godly power and assurance of eternal life. In short, he outlines the steps necessary to making their calling and election sure.

> And beside this, giving all diligence, add to your faith virtue; and to virtue knowledge; And to knowledge temperance; and to temperance patience; and to patience godliness; And to godliness brotherly kindness; and to brotherly kindness charity. For if these things be in you, and abound, they make you that ye shall neither be barren nor unfruitful in the knowledge of our Lord Jesus Christ.

In this way, Peter insists, "[ye shall] make your calling and election sure: for if ye do these things, ye shall never fall" (v. 10).

PETER'S STEPS FOR PARTAKING OF THE DIVINE NATURE

So important are Peter's words that they behoove our careful study. The engine which drives the whole process, Peter declares, is diligence. Because it is possible to escape the powers of the world and gain the divine nature, the Apostle admonishes his readers to give "all diligence."[23] We cannot gain the reward by half-hearted effort or casual performance. We must apply whole-hearted effort to climb the ladder to full knowledge of God and the acquisition of His attributes and power. Elder Marion G. Romney told the Saints that:

> [We] take too much for granted. We assume that because we are members of the Church, we shall receive as a matter of course all the blessings of the gospel. I have heard people contend that they have a claim upon them because they have been through the temple, even though they are not careful to keep the covenants they there made. I do not think this will be the case.

> We might take a lesson from an account given by the Prophet [Joseph Smith] of a vision of the resurrection, in which he records that one of the saddest things he had ever witnessed was the sorrow of members of the Church who came forth to a resurrection below that which they had taken for granted they would receive.[24]

Continued diligence is what gets us to and keeps us on the steps.

Peter begins with the first step: faith. Faith is the starting point of all righteousness. The usage in the Greek reaches beyond mere belief or intellectual assent to include active adherence to the cause believed in. We Latter-day Saints know that the first principle and ordinance of the gospel is "faith in the Lord Jesus Christ" (A of F 4). This is the starting point and we can begin from no other.

Continuing, Peter says, "add to your faith virtue." The Greek word is sometimes translated "goodness," or, as we have seen, "moral excellence." From the earliest sources, the word denoted the idea of skill, the ability to do something well. It was associated with valor in battle. The virtuous man would not run from duty, but fight with such bravery and skill that he was not harmed by the enemy. Peter may have chosen this attribute as his second step in the ladder because he knew of its close association with faith. We must exercise faith—that is, be anxiously engaged in the cause of God—to gain the necessary skills or virtue. As a consequence, it is likely that we will have to stand up for, and perhaps even fight for, what we believe.

Next, Peter admonishes "add to your virtue knowledge." He used the simple form of the Greek noun here.[25] It denotes that knowledge is acquired through study, prayer, faith, and obedience. To those who obey God, the Holy Ghost comes, bringing insight and assurance (see John 14:15–17). As Isaiah said, "Whom shall he teach knowledge? and whom shall he make to understand doctrine? them that are weaned from the milk, and drawn from the breasts. For precept must be upon precept, precept upon precept; line upon line, line upon line; here a little, and there a little" (Isa. 28:9–10). Moroni showed how knowledge, testimony, is dependent on virtue or standing up for what we believe when he said, "for ye receive no witness until after the trial of your faith" (Ether 12:6). Peter, too, knew that knowledge comes only as we battle and serve (see 1 Pet. 1:3–9).

Clearly we do not immediately jump to full knowledge; we gradually grow toward it as we move from the milk of the gospel to the meat through the hard work of service and study, even in the face of opposition. It is at this level that the Holy Ghost escalates His activity in our progression. Therefore, to all who "ask with a sincere heart, with real intent, having faith in Christ, he [God] will manifest the truth of it unto [them], by the power of the Holy Ghost" (Moro. 10:4). Thus, the Spirit will give us knowledge.[26]

Going on, Peter says, "add to knowledge temperance." The Greek combines two words together, "in" and "strength," to form one word carrying the idea of an inner force.[27] The word denotes discipline generally growing out of hard training. Paul states in 1 Corinthians 9:24 that athletes practice temperance, that is, exercise self-control, in order to master a desired skill. Thus, gospel temperance comes as one obeys (practices self-control) with the assistance of the Holy Spirit in order to become like God. The strength within is that of God. It is His power manifesting itself in us through the Holy Ghost. It assists us in overcoming the seductions of false prophets and in living up to our covenants.

Then, says Peter, you must "add to temperance patience." The Greek suggests the idea of remaining true under pressure, thus, translations of "perseverance," "endurance," or "steadfastness" work well. Paul tells us that the race is won not by the swift but by everyone who endures to the finish line (see Heb. 12:1). His example emphasizes the idea that there is no quick road to salvation—the only sure road is one of continued perseverance. He commended the Philippian Saints because "ye have always obeyed, not as in my presence only, but now much more in my absence." However, they could not quit, but must "work out your own salvation with fear and trembling." Persistence in well-doing was still necessary. However, they were not to despair "for it is God which worketh in you both to will and to do of his good pleasure" (Philip. 2:12–13). Note the hope Paul extends to us. We must persevere in righteousness to be saved, but we have God's power working within us to assure our success, though we must be patient and allow the Lord time to make us fully fit.[28]

To this quality, Peter insists that one must "add godliness." The Greek term means devotion to the way of God.[29] But, since faith, virtue, and temperance contain the same idea, Peter probably had a more extensive meaning in mind. In his first epistle, he admonished the Saints to be "holy in all manner of conversation (that is, conduct)."[30] The reason? Because he who "called you is holy," and "because it is written, Be ye holy; for I am holy" (1 Pet. 1:15–16). Here Peter connects the idea of devotion—that is, godliness or proper conduct—with that of holiness. He does so more directly in his second epistle. Describing the Second Coming and the attendant destruction of worldliness, he asks, "What manner of persons ought ye to be in all holy conversation [that is, conduct] and godliness?" (2 Pet. 3:11). Thus, the term "godliness" is, for Peter, directly associated with holy conduct. While many English readers see in holiness the idea of purity, the early Christians saw it in terms of separation, of being set apart from the world.[31]

God wants nothing of this world (meaning the wicked and their ways; see JS–M 1:4). He expects the same from His Saints. John admonished his readers to "love not the world, neither the things that are in the world. If any man love the world, the love of the Father is not in him. For all that is in the world, the lust of the flesh, and the lust of the eyes, and the pride of life, is not of the Father, but is of the world" (1 Jn. 2:15–16). To restate John's idea, he admonishes us not to love the world, for all that is in the world is of the world. We are to be holy, to have no association with the world—to be neither *in* it nor *of* it. Of course, people, both saint and sinner, must live on the earth; but, for John, being in the world is quite a different thing than being on the earth. The world, for him, consists of carnality, avarice, and pride with all its competitiveness. God has nothing to do with these things. Therefore, we must come out of the world—the mundane and the profane—and be separate, to be holy as God is holy.[32]

In short, godliness consists of total devotion to the Lord. We must, in all humility, take upon ourselves God's holy nature and enjoy the associated powers that enable us to keep our covenants. In this way, God will turn our weaknesses into strengths (see Ether 12:27).

THE LAST TWO RUNGS ON PETER'S LADDER

Because godliness covers so many virtues, we might expect it to be the top step of Peter's staircase, but Peter knew otherwise. Two more virtues await those who have become holy. These two virtues push us to concentrate our efforts on others rather than to benefit ourselves. "Add to your godliness," Peter beseeched, "brotherly kindness." The Greek word combines the word for fellowship or brother/sisterhood with that of love. In secular Greek, such love was associated primarily with the family. The early Christians expanded that association to include the community of believers, those who had been born again into God's divine family.

Devotion to God expresses itself in love toward the faithful. John said, "For this is the message that ye heard from the beginning, that we should love one another" (1 Jn. 3:11). Therefore, he warns: "He that saith he is in the light, and hateth his brother, is in darkness even until now. He that loveth his brother abideth in the light, and there is none occasion of stumbling in him. But he that hateth his brother is in darkness, and walketh in darkness, and knoweth not whither he goeth, because that darkness hath blinded his eyes" (1 Jn. 2:9–11).

John associates light with God. He received the association from a good source, the Savior Himself, who taught "that God is light, and in him is no darkness at all" (1 Jn. 1:5). To walk in the light is to walk in the Spirit of God; it is to be enveloped in His capacitating power and the fulness of His love. Those who do so are able, at least in part, to see as God sees, to do as God does, and, most importantly, to feel as God feels. To walk in darkness means to be devoid of God's power and the influence of His Spirit. Those living under such conditions are lost, for they cannot see afar off.

If those walking in darkness are not careful, John warned, something terrible could happen:

> He that loveth not his brother abideth in death. Whosoever hateth his brother is a murderer: and ye know that no murderer hath eternal life abiding in him. Hereby perceive we the love of God, because he laid down his life for us: and we ought to lay down our lives for the brethren. But whoso hath this world's good, and seeth his brother have need, and shutteth up his bowels of compassion from him, how dwelleth the love of God in him? My little children, let us not love in word, neither in tongue; but in deed and in truth (1 Jn. 3:14–18).

John makes two interesting points. First, those who do not have brotherly love are spiritually dead. Further, the lack of sensitivity can lead to hate and to murder. John's use of the term "murder," however, applies not to physical but to spiritual destruction. He uses the term as did Alma the Younger who, when speaking of his rebellious past, confessed that, "I had murdered many of his [God's] children, or rather led them away unto destruction" (Alma 36:14). Those who walk in darkness can come to hate. That, in turn, can cause them to destroy many souls. They will surely destroy their own.

Second, the Savior exemplified the extreme expression of brotherly kindness; He gave His life that others might live. John insists that Christians must be prepared to do the same. Considering that, as he wrote, the Lord's disciples, both men and women, were being killed by Roman pagans, his words were more than metaphors.

However, the chance that a person would actually have to give his life for the Church, even in times of heavy persecution, was slight. But giving one's life does not have to mean martyrdom. John had a better way of giving one's life—through service. To do so takes the ability to see through eyes of love. When we see a brother or sister in need, our job is to respond. Of course, few have unlimited resources (thus John's qualifier, "but whoso hath this world's good"), but all can do something, even if it is no more than giving sympathy, caring, and prayer. When we do this out of a pure heart, we can say, as did John, "We know that we have passed from death unto life, because we love the brethren" (1 Jn. 3:14). So John gives us an important key way to gauge if we have been born again into eternal life. We simply have to ask, "How much do I love others?" (I will develop this theme more fully in the next chapter.)

Note that, as important as brotherly kindness is, it still does not bring us to the top step of Peter's ladder. His last step reveals a love that transcends even saintly love. The Savior said, "Ye have heard that it hath been said, Thou shalt love they neighbour, and hate thine enemy. But I say unto you, Love your enemies, bless them that curse you, do good to them that hate you, and pray from them which despitefully use you, and persecute you; That ye may be the children of your Father which is in heaven. . . . For if ye love them which love you, what reward have ye?" (Matt. 5:43–46).

It is with this understanding that Peter admonishes the Saints to "add to brotherly kindness charity." The English word charity, fortunately, does help us understand Peter's intent.[33] The Greek word denotes that feeling of benevolent goodwill toward humankind in general, which translates itself into kindly liberality and helpfulness. The Greek word could be translated simply as "pure love." It expresses, as we have seen, a love that gives freely, asking nothing in return, not even appreciation or recognition. Such is the quality of God's love.

Those possessed of that kind of love center their lives in service to others. They are neither in the world nor of the world, with all its hate, avarice, pride, and lust. Through love they have escaped the world, and they dwell in God. (Again, we will study more of this in the next chapter.)

Thus, Peter promises that "if these things be in you, and abound, they make you that ye shall neither be barren nor unfruitful in the knowledge of our Lord Jesus Christ" (2 Pet. 1:8). Here, at the end, he again uses the intense form of the noun "knowledge."[34] Those who have the attributes he describes know God, not because they have seen or touched or walked with Him, but because they are somewhat like Him in thought, action, and feeling. His light and spirit dwell in them. Sight and sound, as witnesses of God, fall far behind those of the indwelling power of the Spirit.

We make our election sure in this way because, possessing these attributes, we will never fail in our duty. We have done, we now do, and we will always do all that God requires. Consequently, the Holy Spirit seals us into eternal life. This is what Peter meant when he admonished the Saints to make their calling and election sure. Those who have done these things fulfill all that God requires and, for that, He guarantees them eternal life based on continued diligence.

A DEFINITION OF "THE MORE SURE WORD OF PROPHECY"

Associated with the idea of making one's calling sure is something called "the more sure word of prophecy." Many have heard this phrase used and wondered where it comes from and what it means. The phrase is found in the writings of Peter. There the prophet bears his testimony to his readers that:

> [We] have not followed cunningly devised fables, when we made known unto you the power and coming of our Lord Jesus Christ, but were eyewitnesses of his majesty. For he received from God the Father honour and glory, when there came such a voice to him from the excellent glory, This is my beloved Son, in whom I am well pleased. And this voice which came from heaven we heard, when we were with him in the holy mount. We have also a more sure word of prophecy; whereunto ye do well that ye take heed, as unto a light that shineth in a dark place, until the day dawn, and the day star arise in your hearts (2 Pet. 1:16–19).

Note the power of Peter's testimony. He reminds his readers of the time when He, with John and James, saw the Savior transfigured (see Matt. 17:1–9). Peter testifies that he not only saw the glory of the Christ, but that he also heard God proclaim His divine paternity of, and delight in, His noble Son. This witness, Peter stressed, became a "more sure word of prophecy"; in other words, it made certain the prophecies of the Old Testament.[35] The Joseph Smith Translation underscores this idea. It reads: "We have therefore a more sure knowledge of the word of prophecy, to which word of prophecy ye do well that ye take heed" (JST, 2 Pet. 1:19). God's revelation to the three leaders affirmed the Old Testament witness concerning the Messiah and His saving ministry.

John Taylor explained the idea of the more sure word of prophecy in these words:

> When we come to investigate the things that God makes manifest in our own day through the living oracles, that in spirit and in doctrine they correspond with the things that God revealed in days of old. We, then, have "a more sure word of prophecy" than the things that were written aforetime. The Apostle Peter spoke of this in his day. He said that holy men of God wrote and spoke as they were moved upon by the Holy Ghost, and that no prophecy of the Scripture is of any private interpretation. He said further, "We have also a more sure word of prophecy; whereunto ye do well that ye take heed, as unto a light that shineth in a dark place, until the day dawn, and the day star arise in your hearts." They had the living oracles. The people who lived in Peter's day had not only the words of Isaiah, Jeremiah, Ezekiel and the other prophets, and the Book of the Laws, as written by Moses, the inspired prophet of God, who looked upon God and talked with Him face-to-face— they not only had these things written in the ancient records, but they had living oracles, men in their midst who were authorized to speak in the name of the Lord and declare to the people the living word of God for their present benefit. And as it was with the people in that day, so

it is in this Church that Jesus Christ our Savior has re-established on the earth. We have the living oracles, those who are called and ordained to stand between us and the Lord.[36]

Brigham Young gave a good example of how the Church today possesses a more sure word of prophecy than even those living in Peter's day. He taught the Saints that the early Apostles were mistaken in a few things:

> There can be no doubt but they were mistaken with regard to the time of the winding up scene, thinking it was much nearer than it really was, and they might have made mistakes in other respects. Many of the difficulties they had to encounter, we are not troubled with. We have not only the sure word of prophecy delivered in the days of the Apostles, but we actually have that surer word of prophecy delivered to us through the Prophet Joseph, that in the last days the Lord would gather Israel, build up Zion, and establish His kingdom upon the earth. This is a more sure word of prophecy than was delivered in the days of the Apostles, and is a greater work than they had to perform.[37]

These two quotes explain perfectly the context of 2 Peter where it speaks of "the more sure word of prophecy."

It is important to keep in mind the relationship between making one's calling and election sure and the more sure word of prophecy in the context of 2 Peter. That text does not admonish the Saints to receive the more sure word of prophecy. It says that Peter received it, and the Saints should heed his testimony until they receive a sure knowledge or testimony for themselves (see 2 Pet.1:19). Now he does admonish them to make sure of their calling and election by acquiring the attributes he listed, the greatest of these being love, but he does not say anything directly about receiving the more sure word. For him, the Saint achieves eternal life by adding virtue to virtue, gaining a sure testimony, and continuing in all diligence. He knows that these are all God requires. Even saying that, however, the tale is not fully told.

ANOTHER DEFINITION OF "THE MORE SURE WORD
OF PROPHECY"

In order to understand the whole concept, we must turn to insights from the Restoration. According to Doctrine and Covenants 131:5, "The more sure word of prophecy means a man's knowing that he is sealed up unto eternal life, by revelation and the spirit of prophecy, through the power of the Holy Priesthood." This scripture links making one's calling and election sure with receiving the more sure word of prophecy[38]. Only when one receives this revelation associated with the powers of the priesthood is the promise of eternal life made unconditional or, in other words, sure.

Explaining why priesthood authority is necessary, the Lord said that the Melchizedek "priesthood administereth the gospel and holdeth the key of the mysteries of the kingdom, even the key of the knowledge of God. Therefore, in the ordinances thereof, the power of godliness is manifest. And without the ordinances thereof, and the authority of the priesthood, the power of godliness is not manifest unto men in the flesh; For without this no man can see the face of God, even the Father, and live" (D&C 84:19–22). Through priesthood ordinances, the recipient gains knowledge of God and receives the power of godliness, that is, the power to live "godly lives. It is the power of godly men and godly women, through the ordinances of the Priesthood."[39] When people live godly lives, they put themselves in a position to receive all the Father has. He states very clearly that "I am bound when ye do what I say" (D&C 82:10); as a result, eternal life follows diligence.

Through inspiration, Joseph Smith revealed an insight into Peter's teachings dealing with calling and election. He told the Saints:

> Now, there is some grand secret here, and keys to unlock the subject. Notwithstanding the apostle exhorts them to add to their faith, virtue, knowledge, temperance, etc., yet he exhorts them to make their calling and election sure. And though they had heard an audible voice from heaven bearing testimony that Jesus was the Son of God, yet he says we have a more sure word of prophecy, whereunto ye do well that ye take heed as unto a light shining in a dark

place. Now, wherein could they have a more sure word of prophecy than to hear the voice of God saying, This is my beloved Son.

Now for the secret and grand key. Though they might hear the voice of God and know that Jesus was the Son of God, this would be no evidence that their election and calling was made sure, that they had part with Christ, and were joint heirs with Him. They then would want that more sure word of prophecy, that they were sealed in the heavens and had the promise of eternal life in the kingdom of God.[40]

So the "more sure word" confirmed that they, too, were sealed into heaven and would receive eternal life. What many overlook is that this prophetic word did not actually seal Peter, James, and John. It confirmed a sealing that had already taken place. Many people do not seem to understand that we must first become called, elected, and sealed *before* we will ever receive the more sure word of prophecy. The more sure word merely confirms what the Spirit has already done.

I fear some overly zealous souls get the cart before the horse. What we should be concerned about is not receiving the revelation but living in such a way that the Holy Spirit is active in our lives. "*The Holy Spirit of Promise*," according to Joseph Fielding Smith, "*is the Holy Ghost* who places the stamp of approval upon every ordinance: baptism, confirmation, ordination, marriage. *The promise is that the blessings will be received through faithfulness.*"[41]

The more sure word of prophecy does two things: it confirms the sealing that has already taken place, and it makes the blessings sure.[42] What it does not do is confer those blessings in the first place. What I want to emphasize is that we usually become the called and elect of God long before the Lord decides to give us the confirming revelation. It is in this light that Elder Harold B. Lee told the Saints, "Although not seeing, yet believing, we rejoice with joy unspeakable in receiving the end of our faith, even the salvation of our souls."[43] Though we may not have had the word confirmed upon us, we can be assured that through faithfulness the blessing will come.

We must also understand that blessings flow from the conditional sealing. We do not have to wait for the more sure word to enjoy the blessings of faithfulness. The Lord explained to the early members of the Church that the Holy Spirit of Promise would seal them "up unto the day of redemption, that ye may not fall notwithstanding the hour of temptation that may come upon you" (D&C 124:124). The sealing blessing comes to those "who overcome by faith" and "are just and true" (D&C 76:53). That is what occurs when we have the Spirit in our lives.

The sealing by the Holy Spirit of Promise is not contingent on the more sure word of prophecy, but is given to all who are faithful in keeping God's commandments. What motivates them to do so? The Savior supplied the answer: "If a man love me, he will keep my words" (John 14:23). Jude admonished the Saints to "keep yourselves in the love of God, looking for the mercy of our Lord Jesus Christ unto eternal life" (Jude 1:21). The word "keep" means "to watch over," "protect," and "guard."[44] Thus, he admonished the people to avoid straying outside the boundaries of their love for God. As long as they remain in those boundaries they will never fall.

When we so protect ourselves, we receive a tremendous promise: "Ye shall abide in my love" the Savior declared; "even as I have kept my Father's commandments, and abide in his love" (John 15:10). This blessing from the Lord acts as a guardian of our eternal lives, empowering us to get through temptations' trials. Charity, the pure love of Christ, never fails (see 1 Cor. 13:8). Therefore, "whoso keepeth his word, in him verily is the love of God perfected: hereby know we that we are in him" (1 Jn. 2:5). The reason is that "God is love; and he that dwelleth in love dwelleth in God, and God in him. Herein is our love made perfect, that we may have boldness in the day of judgment: because as he is, so are we in this world" (1 Jn. 4:16–17). Because pure love is our assurance that we will receive eternal life, it is one of God's greatest gifts. It not only assists us in overcoming temptations but also allows us to fully know him because "God is love" (1 Jn. 4:8).

THE FRUIT ON LEHI'S TREE OF LIFE

This brings us, once again, to the vision of Lehi and the question we have been exploring: What does the fruit of the tree represent?

Lehi partook of the fruit of the tree of love and it filled him with joy. That fruit seems to represent the sealing power of the Holy Spirit of Promise as it flows from the love of God. Lehi partook of that power and out of it grew an even more pure and perfect love that filled his soul with joy. The effect on him was most telling. He wanted to share what he had with others. Lehi had no desire to hoard the fruit or save it just for himself, and it never crossed his mind to profit from it. Instead, he simply wanted to share all he had found with others. The fruit has this effect on people.

By sharing the pure love of Christ, we can make our calling and election sure. A statement by Joseph Smith supports this idea: "Until we have perfect love we are liable to fall." Like Peter, Paul, and John, he knew that love guards against rebellion and apostasy. He continued, "When we have a testimony that our names are sealed in the Lamb's book of life we have perfect love and then it is impossible for false Christs to deceive us."[45]

The operative word here is "sealed." The Prophet did not say "written." The Lamb writes the Saints' names in His book when they have sacrificed for the kingdom and pushed forward its cause unselfishly.[46] In this way, they have their names conditionally recorded in the Lamb's book of life while yet in mortality (Luke 10:20). If they transgress, their names are blotted out, and they lose their reward (Rev. 3:5; 22:19; Alma 5:57; D&C 85:5, 11). Ultimately, only the names of those who qualify for eternal life are "sealed" in the Lamb's book. The Prophet states that a person can have a testimony that this has happened. That confirmation we call "the more sure word of prophecy."

Based on what Joseph Smith said, we may assume that Lehi's name was sealed in the Lamb's book of life. The ancient prophet certainly knew that "the Lord hath redeemed my soul from hell; I have beheld his glory, and I am encircled about eternally in the arms of his love" (2 Ne. 1:15). Such knowledge would fill any righteous soul with joy.

Certain blessings flow out of this sealing. One of these is that the participant receives perfect love.[47] The two go together: one cannot receive the sealing without love, and one cannot receive a perfect love without the sealing. The sealing itself does not bring love, but rather perfected love. In becoming sealed, we must have already exercised and grown in our love toward God and His children. We must have partaken of the fruit of the tree so that all our love needs is the final perfecting touch. Once that touch is added, we will never fall.

THE GREAT AND SPACIOUS BUILDING

Unfortunately, there is a downside to partaking of the fruit. Lehi pointed it out. He tells us that he saw, not far from where the tree grew, a "great and spacious" building whose inhabitants wore "exceedingly fine" dress. These people jeered and mocked those who had partaken of the fruit of the tree. Some of those who had tasted of the fruit "were ashamed, because of those that were scoffing at them; and they fell away into forbidden paths and were lost" (1 Ne. 8:26--28). Partaking of the fruit did not save these people. Instead, it brought upon them a sure death.

The problem was that they turned away from the tree of love too soon, before their love could be perfected. As their love moved toward perfection, opposition arose. The pressure from the world became terrible, and eventually they yielded. Even though their names were sealed in the Lamb's book of life, they could not be safeguarded against certain sins. The Prophet Joseph Smith taught the Saints that:

> [The] doctrine that the Presbyterians and Methodists have quarreled so much about—once in grace, always in grace, or falling away from grace, I will say a word about. They are both wrong. Truth takes a road between them both, for while the Presbyterian says: "Once in grace, you cannot fall"; the Methodist says: "You can have grace today, fall from it tomorrow, next day have grace again; and so follow on, changing continually." But the doctrine of the Scriptures and the spirit of Elijah would show them both false, and take a road between them both; for, according to the Scripture, if men have received the good word of God, and tasted of the powers of the world to come, if they shall fall away, it is impossible to renew them again, seeing they have crucified the Son of God afresh, and put Him to an

open shame; so there is a possibility of falling away; you could not be renewed again, and the power of Elijah cannot seal against this sin, for this is a reserve made in the seals and power of the Priesthood.[48]

This is the case with those in Lehi's vision who could not endure in faith, but apostatized from the truth and fell into forbidden paths.[49] The world got to them before love could perfect them and keep them from ever falling. This tragedy should not frighten us, only put us on guard. Most of those who made their way to the tree remained, allowing their love to become perfected and their eternal life assured.

THE EFFECT OF THE FRUIT OF LOVE

Good things happen when people partake of the fruit of love. Remember the prophet Enos? He went out to the woods to hunt, but instead found himself praying for and receiving forgiveness of sins. What motivated him, he says, was "the words which I had often heard my father speak concerning eternal life, and the joy of the saints" (Enos 1:3). It is interesting that his hunger for life and joy brought forgiveness of sin, but that alone did not satisfy Enos. Once he received forgiveness, he continued to pray for the welfare of others. Why? What was his motive? Admittedly, the account never mentions the word "love." Faith gets all the credit, as well it should. We must not, however, overlook the feelings of his heart—for he says that once he had received forgiveness, he "began to feel a desire for the welfare of my brethren, the Nephites" (Enos 1:9). That desire for the welfare of his friends, though unnamed, could be nothing less than love, that same love that impelled him to ask for blessings even upon his foes (see Enos 1:11–12). It is this love that lifts, inspires, and encompasses, never growing tired of well doing. No wonder those who are filled with perfect love have their names sealed in the Lamb's book of life and will never fall.

The scriptures give ample witness of those who made their calling and election sure through loving service, thereafter receiving the more sure word of prophecy. The Book of Mormon tells us that Enos, in addition to Lehi, received a witness. He testified, "I soon go to the place of my rest, which is with my Redeemer; for I know that in him I shall rest. And I rejoice in the day when my mortal shall put on immortality, and shall stand before him; then shall I see his face with pleasure, and he will say unto me: Come unto me, ye blessed, there is a place prepared for you in the mansions of my Father" (Enos 1:27).

In response to a prayer concerning the administration of the Church, the voice of the Lord came to Alma the Elder, saying, "I covenant with thee that thou shalt have eternal life" (Mosiah 26:20). Then, in 3 Nephi, the Savior sealed up His Nephite disciples, saying, "After that ye are seventy and two years old ye shall come unto me in my kingdom; and with me ye shall find rest" (3 Ne. 28:3). To Moroni, the Lord promised, "Thou hast been faithful; wherefore, thy garments shall be made clean. And because thou hast seen thy weakness thou shalt be made strong, even unto the sitting down in the place which I have prepared in the mansions of my Father" (Ether 12:37).

The Bible gives us the example of Paul, who also partook of the fruit of love. He wrote to his friend Timothy, "I endure all things for the elect's sakes, that they may also obtain the salvation which is in Christ Jesus with eternal glory" (2 Tim. 2:10). Note the power in the use of the little word, "also." He goes on to say more clearly that "I have fought a good fight, I have finished my course, I have kept the faith: Henceforth there is laid up for me a crown of righteousness, which the Lord, the righteous judge, shall give me at that day: and not to me only, but unto all them also that love his appearing" (2 Tim. 4:7–8). Finally, he testified that the Lord "will preserve me unto his heavenly kingdom" (2 Tim. 4:18).

In modern times, we find the principle still operating. As noted above, the Lord assured those who were present with Joseph Smith when the "Olive Leaf" revelation (section 88) was given that they would have eternal life. To Joseph Smith the Lord promised that "[I] will be with thee even unto the end of the world, and through all eternity; for verily I seal upon you your exaltation, and prepare a throne for you in the kingdom of my Father" (D&C 132:49).

SEALED BY THE HOLY SPIRIT OF PROMISE

So what about "ordinary" members of the Church, people who are never called as general authorities or prophets? Do such things happen to them? Though receiving the more sure word of prophecy is the only way we can know that our blessings have been *unconditionally* sealed upon us, there is a way we can know that they are *conditionally* sealed and operating. Paul assured the faithful Ephesians that, because of their faithfulness, they were "sealed with that holy Spirit of promise." He says that this sealing was the "earnest" of their celestial inheritance (Eph. 1:13–14).

The Greek word translated as "earnest," in its secular sense, refers to a down payment that secures a person's legal claim to a desired object. The word also describes the payment which seals an agreement and obligates a contracting party to pay the contracted amount in full.[50] Paul adopted the word and, in a figurative sense, used it to define a function of the Holy Spirit. In his model, God is the contracting party because He is the one with whom the Saint makes a covenant. The terms of the contract are simple: the Saint promises obedience, and God promises eternal life. As assurance to the Saint that he will get his reward, God gives the Holy Ghost as a spiritual pledge, or earnest deposit, as it were, on forthcoming celestial glory.

It is in this light that Paul can say that God "hath also sealed us, and given the earnest of the Spirit in our hearts" (2 Cor. 1:22). The Spirit acts as the assurance that a sealing of our future blessings has taken place, and we will eventually receive the full payment of eternal life. Paul reinforced the idea by telling the Saints that God brought them into the gospel that they might receive eternal life and "also hath given unto us the earnest of the Spirit" (2 Cor. 5:5). It appears that they had not yet received the more sure word of prophecy. Therefore, their sealing was still conditional. Nonetheless, the Spirit assured them that the sealing was intact, and, if it remained that way, God would give them the fulness of the promised reward.

Even for us today, the Spirit is the earnest of our salvation. Those moments when we feel the soft touch of the Spirit are God's sweet testimony of our continued sealing. Our task is to keep the Spirit. That requires more than maintaining the status quo. The simple, if gracious, acts that kept the Spirit active in our lives in the past may not be enough for the future. What we must do to assure its continued presence is mature further in the gospel, make and keep sacred covenants, render more service, become more godly and acquire more love, always remembering that "as many as are led by the Spirit of God" are the children of God and the heirs of His glory (Rom. 8:14–17). Should we offend the Spirit, our Father-child relationship with God is absolved until deep repentance restores it once more.

Those who seek to assure themselves of eternal life without continued service, persistent endurance, faithfulness, self-sacrifice, and ever greater expressions of love, seek a myth they shall never realize. The more sure word of prophecy is no shortcut to heaven.[51]

CONCLUSION

In His vision to Lehi, God brought together three primary elements associated with salvation: love, calling and election, and joy. Let's look at the interrelationship of each. Lehi's tree represented the love of God the Father, particularly that love which allowed Him to send His Son. At the same time, it represents the Son's love shown through both service and the Atonement. Because of these gifts of love, as John testified, "now are we the sons [and daughters] of God." He admitted that "it doth not yet appear what we shall be: but we know that, when he shall appear, we shall be like him; for we shall see him as he is" (1 Jn. 3:2). Note the force of the word "now." God's judgment is already in force upon the faithful. Using His authority,[52] the Lord decides our case while we are yet in mortality. Here and now we become His sons and daughters, being sealed by the Holy Spirit of Promise. When we die, we return to God in His eternal realm.

Thus, through the power of God's love and through the reciprocating power in us, we make our calling and election to celestial glory sure. The more sure word of prophecy is but a by-product of that love. We do not have to worry about the more sure word. It will come if and when God decides. Our task is to walk the path, holding on to the iron rod, come to the tree, partake of its fruit, and allow God to perfect our love. We may not receive the more sure word of prophecy in mortality, but we can receive the Holy Spirit of Promise, which is the pledge, or as Paul says, "the earnest," of our future inheritance. Celestial joy will come as we gain the love of Christ, for "all things work together for good to them that love God, to them who are the called according to his purpose" (Rom. 8:28).

CHAPTER 7
THE COMMANDMENT *to* LOVE

In his vision, Lehi partook of the fruit of the tree representing God's love, and in doing so became filled with joy. Lehi seems to have been touched with a divine quality of love, for he wanted desperately to share his joy with others. There is a lesson here: if we would find joy, we must not only acquire divine love, but we, too, must want to share it with others. As a matter of fact, the New Testament commands us to do so.

THE LOVE COMMANDMENT

On three different occasions, people asked the Savior which of all the commandments was the greatest. Behind the question lay decades of debate and argument among Jewish authorities. It was probably for that reason that many sought for *the*—not *an*—answer and were sensitive to those who might be able to provide it. On one occasion, a good-hearted scribe witnessed the Savior skillfully answer the probing questions of a malevolent group of Pharisees and Sadducees. Mark tells us that "having heard them reasoning together, and perceiving that he had answered them well, [the scribe] asked him, Which is the first commandment of all? And Jesus answered him, The first of all the commandments is, Hear, O Israel; The Lord our God is one Lord" (Mark 12:28–29). It is of interest that the Savior began answering the question by quoting Deuteronomy 6:4. One could jump to the conclusion that the great commandment was the first listed in the Decalogue: "Thou shalt have no other gods before me" (Ex. 20:3). But that is not the case; taking the scripture in context, the Savior finishes, "And thou shalt love the Lord thy God with all thy heart, and with all thy soul, and with all thy mind, and with all thy strength" (Deut. 6:5; Mark 12:30).

It was Moses who bound the commandment to love God with a statement underscoring Jehovah's oneness. What Moses emphasized to Israel, as the foundation for their devotion to the Lord, was that Jehovah, their only God, has integrity. Alma put forth the same idea, saying that God "cannot walk in crooked paths; neither doth he vary from that which he hath said; neither hath he a shadow of turning from the right to the left, or from that which is right to that which is wrong; therefore, his course is one eternal round" (Alma 7:20). His constancy in righteousness makes God the proper object of our love.

The Savior, however, was not finished answering the scribe's question. Going on, he added:

> And the second is like, namely this, Thou shalt love thy neighbour as thyself. There is none other commandment greater than these. And the scribe said unto him, Well, Master, thou hast said the truth: for there is one God; and there is none other but he: And to love him with all the heart, and with all the understanding, and with all the soul, and with all the strength, and to love his neighbour as himself, is more than all whole burnt offerings and sacrifices. And when Jesus saw that he answered discreetly, he said unto him, Thou art not far from the kingdom of God. And no man after that durst ask him any question (Mark 12:31–34).

On the surface, it seems a bit surprising that the Lord gave the scribe two answers when he expected only one. However, the question demanded a full answer, and that answer had an A and a B part. God's greatest commandment consists in loving Him and allowing that love to overflow to His children, including oneself.

Consider that last point for a moment. God has told us that we are to love Him with heart, might, mind, and strength. With that He has given us a standard by which to judge our love for Him. What is the standard for loving a neighbor? God said we are to love him as we love ourselves. If we have no self-love, no self-respect, we have no standard to gauge our love for others. Therefore, it is very important to God that His children learn to love themselves.

THE DANGER OF PRIDE

Of course, there is a danger here. If we are not careful, we can move easily from self-respect to self-conceit, from appreciation of self to pride, from assisting others to competition against all. Indeed, modern prophets have warned us against it. President Ezra Taft Benson soberly admonishes us that:

> [I]n the scriptures there is no such thing as righteous pride. It is always considered as a sin. We are not speaking of a wholesome view of self-worth, which is best established by a close relationship with God. But we are speaking of pride as the universal sin, as someone has described it. Mormon writes that "the pride of this nation, or the people of the Nephites, hath proven their destruction" (Moroni 8:27). The Lord says in the Doctrine and Covenants, "Beware of pride, lest ye become as the Nephites of old" (D&C 38:39). Essentially, pride is a "my will" rather than "thy will" approach to life. The opposite of pride is humbleness, meekness, submissiveness, or teachableness (see Alma 13:28).
>
> Pride does not look up to God and care about what is right. It looks sideways to man and argues who is right. Pride is manifest in the spirit of contention. Was it not through pride that the devil became the devil? Christ wanted to serve. The devil wanted to rule. Christ wanted to bring men to where He was. The devil wanted to be above men. Christ removed self as the force in His perfect life. It was not my will, but thine be done (see Mark 14:36; Luke 22:42).[1]

What guards against overstepping God's bounds and moving into pride is true love—manifested in a genuine care for self and others.

When this happens, we develop humility, that virtue exactly opposite the vice of pride. And God very much wants us to be humble. Indeed, he has promised that "if my people, which are called by my name, shall humble themselves, and pray, and seek my face, and turn from their wicked ways; then will I hear from heaven, and will forgive their sin" (2 Chr. 7:14). Jesus stated, "Whosoever therefore shall humble himself as this little child, the same is greatest in the kingdom of heaven" (Matt. 18:4).

ON HUMILITY

What we must understand clearly is that God does not condemn pride because it threatens Him or command humility as something due to His dignity, as though God suffered from pride. He is not the least bit worried about His station or dignity. He is worried about us and what might throw us out of His reach. Humility is His means of bringing us to Him, of allowing us to get in touch with Him. And, as C. S. Lewis writes, whenever we do get in touch with Him, we will be "delightedly humble, feeling the infinite relief of having for once got rid of all the silly nonsense about your own dignity which has made you restless and unhappy all your life. He is trying to make you humble in order to make this moment possible: trying to take off a lot of silly, ugly, fancy-dress in which we have all got ourselves up and are strutting about like the little idiots we are."[2]

It is unfortunate that this virtue has come to be synonymous for self-depreciation and abjectness. That definition throws us off so that we are unable to see models of this virtue. Again, quoting from Lewis:

> Do not imagine that if you meet a really humble man he will be what most people call "humble" nowadays: he will not be a sort of greasy, smarmy person, who is always telling you that, of course, he is nobody. Probably all you will think about him is that he seemed a cheerful, intelligent chap who took a real interest in what you said to him. If you do dislike him it will be because you feel a little envious of anyone who seems to enjoy life so easily. He will not be thinking about humility: he will not be thinking about himself at all.[3]

Let me stress the point I am making here. Humility, an aspect of self-love, allows us to concentrate on others because we are secure with ourselves. It allows us, as Elder Neal A. Maxwell has written, to cultivate

> in ourselves not only love and interest in others, but also a genuine curiosity—the kind of love which seeks to know. G. K. Chesterton asserts in his book *Orthodoxy* "how much larger your life would be if your self were smaller in it; if you could really look at other men with common curiosity and pleasure. . . . You would begin to be interested in them. . . . You would break out of this tiny and tawdry theatre in which your own little plot is always being played, and you would find yourself under a freer sky, and in a street full of splendid strangers."[4]

That is the beauty of love; it frees us from the slavery of self. We find both freedom and joy in others. The result is a genuine outreach to them.

To whom do we extend that reach? The answer lies in the Lord's response to one who asked concerning the requirements for eternal life. This time, the inquirer was not good-hearted; he was a lawyer who put forth his question in an attempt to discredit and perhaps embarrass the Lord. He said,

> Master, what shall I do to inherit eternal life? He said unto him, What is written in the law? how readest thou? And he answering said, Thou shalt love the Lord thy God with all thy heart, and with all thy soul, and with all thy strength, and with all thy mind; and thy neighbour as thyself. And he said unto him, Thou hast answered right: this do, and thou shalt live. But He, willing to justify himself, said unto Jesus, And who is my neighbour? (Luke 10:25–29).

Note that the lawyer had the correct answer. The Savior may have known that and allowed him to reinforce the Savior's own doctrine.

All this must have been quite embarrassing for the lawyer and he sought "to justify himself" by quickly asking another question. We can question his sincerity in wanting an answer. Still, the Lord obliged by telling the parable of the good Samaritan who helped a Jew wounded by thieves when a Levite and Priest would not. The Savior then followed the story up with the question of his own: "Which now of these three, thinkest thou, was neighbour unto him that fell among the thieves? And he said, He that shewed mercy on him. Then said Jesus unto him, Go, and do thou likewise" (Luke 10:36–37).

LOVE THY NEIGHBOR

Through this story, Luke provides us with a salutary reminder of what love really means. Many of us seem totally prepared to love God in some nebulous, ethereal way that lets us get away without having the depth of our commitment really plumbed. This is what makes the position attractive. It becomes only as demanding as we allow it to be, and, more importantly, is rarely tested in actual practice. However, the command to love our neighbor presents a very different standard—one that is very concrete, tremendously demanding, and quite easy to measure. It expects attention to service—much of which can be quite unpleasant and sometimes a thing we would, naturally, rather not perform—but it may be these very properties that balance "love thy neighbor" with "love God" in the great commandment.[5]

Allow me to illustrate. Some overzealous souls have stressed the importance of obtaining some mystical love relationship with the Savior or the Father. The attempt often causes a quasi-spiritual emotionalism resulting in a search for God through a deep, otherworldly piety, but that is not what the scriptures teach. They insist that we find God not through mysticism and withdrawal, but through love and involvement. There is an organic tie between love for God and love of His children that precludes sinking into the depths of oneself.[6] That tie insists on service to one's neighbor. President Harold B. Lee reported having heard President David O. McKay teach that "if you want to love God, you have to learn to love and serve the people. That is the way you show your love for God."[7]

Another point in the Lord's interaction with the lawyer is very interesting: the Savior never answered the lawyer's question. There is little wonder. The question "Who is my neighbor?" was drawn from a selfish and prideful heart and did not deserve an answer. The lawyer wanted the Lord to define the limits of love, to reveal the minimum the Lord expected of His disciples.

The Savior did, however, answer another question, the one the lawyer should have asked. Simply stated, it is, "How can I show myself a true neighbor?" Here we see, in grand contrast, the Savior's doctrine compared to that of the scribes and lawyers. They debated endlessly concerning the area bounded by love, how long the string measuring love's radius should be, who should be included and who excluded. The Savior cut the string, showing that love should flow endlessly outward to include anyone we can help or care about.[8]

We see the same thing in the Savior's commandments. As Jehovah, He commanded Israel to love not only those of their own race (see Lev. 19:18), but also the resident alien (see Lev. 19:34). The commandment not only revealed the heart of the Israelite religion but also that of God, who Himself practices that very kind of love (see Deut. 10:18). The point is that the Lord shows the way by first loving us and kindling love in us. John understood this. He said, "we love him, because he first loved us" (1 Jn. 4:19). John is not saying that we love out of gratitude to God for His love for us, nor is he saying that we love in imitation of God's love. He is saying that God's love creates love in us.[9]

However, God can produce love in us only if we desire and are willing to receive it. As the Lord said in Doctrine and Covenants 88:33, "For what doth it profit a man if a gift is bestowed upon him, and he receive not the gift? Behold, he rejoices not in that which is given unto him, neither rejoices in him who is the giver of the gift." Perhaps that is one of the reasons Moroni taught his readers that "charity is the pure love of Christ, and it endureth forever; and whoso is found possessed of it at the last day, it shall be well with him," and admonished them to "pray unto the Father with all the energy of heart, that ye may be filled with this love, which he hath bestowed upon all who are true followers of his Son, Jesus Christ; that ye may become the sons of God" (Moro. 7:47–48).

Consider the story of the rich young ruler who asked the Savior, "What good thing shall I do, that I may have eternal life?" The Lord responded, "If thou wilt enter into life, keep the commandments." To the young man's inquiry, "Which?" the Lord answered, "Thou shalt do no murder, Thou shalt not commit adultery, Thou shalt not steal, Thou shalt not bear false witness, Honour thy father and thy mother: and, Thou shalt love thy neighbour as thyself" (Matt. 19:16–19). The Lord's answer reached beyond the Ten Commandments to include the foundation from which they sprang—love of neighbor.

The young ruler's response is quite arresting. He said, "All these things have I kept from my youth up: what lack I yet?" (Matt. 19:20). His bold statement, as startling as it might appear, was spoken without guile—he truly believed he had fulfilled the law. And the Lord's reaction, as expressed by Mark is also arresting. "Then Jesus beholding him loved him" (Mark 10:21). Mark's point is that what follows next grew out of the Savior's profound love for this young ruler. The Lord "said unto him, One thing thou lackest: go thy way, sell whatsoever thou hast, and give to the poor, and thou shalt have treasure in heaven: and come, take up the cross, and follow me" (Mark 10:21).

"One thing thou lackest." What an interesting phrase. The man was truly close to heaven, lacking but one thing. And what was that one thing? Love of neighbor. The Lord had included that in his list of commandments, and the young man felt, quite honestly it seems, that he had been living it, but now it was showtime. He had to demonstrate neighborly love, not as he chose, but as God demanded. The result? He "went away grieved: for he had great possessions" (Mark 10:22). You see, he was self-deluded. He had been loving God and his fellow men according to his own standard, not God's. The Master's request stripped away his self-deception and allowed the man to see just how little he was really willing to pay for eternal life, as well as disclosing the real cost of loving one's neighbor.

Another point this incident underscores is, as the Savior said, "No man can serve two masters: for either he will hate the one, and love the other; or else he will hold to the one, and despise the other. Ye cannot serve God and mammon" (Matt. 6:24). *Mammon* is an Aramaic term meaning "property" or "wealth."[10] However, the Lord's teaching should not be construed to mean that a person cannot be both wealthy and faithful. The problem is not wealth, but service. One cannot be faithful to God and devote himself to gaining riches.[11]

There is good reason. Humans are not capable of loving and serving two different masters, each of whom demand total allegiance. The heart becomes the key to devotion, and devotion the key to service. The Lord counseled, "Lay not up for yourselves treasures upon earth, where moth and rust doth corrupt, and where thieves break through and steal: But lay up for yourselves treasures in heaven, where neither moth nor rust doth corrupt, and where thieves do not break through nor steal: For where your treasure is, there will your heart be also" (Matt. 6:19–21). What we treasure, we love. God demands that we treasure Him first and foremost. To push the point, He is to be our first love.

THE PURPOSE OF THE GIFTS OF THE SPIRIT

To those who love Him, God gives His greatest gifts. These He expects His children to use in blessing others here on the earth. We commonly call these the gifts of the Spirit. He says, speaking of them, "always remembering for what they are given; For verily I say unto you, they are given for the benefit of those who love me and keep all my commandments, and him that seeketh so to do; that all may be benefited that seek or that ask of me" (D&C 46:8–9). The twin virtues of love and service are directly associate with God's gifts. The Lord explains why when He says, "I would that ye should always remember, and always retain in your minds what those gifts are, that are given unto the church. For all have not every gift given unto them; for there are many gifts, and to every man is given a gift by the Spirit of God. To some is given one, and to some is given another, that all may be profited thereby" (D&C 46: 10–12). The gifts are for those who, like God, have separated themselves from the materialistic values of the world, and have devoted themselves, again like God, to the service of His children.

In this light, consider another point. All of us, at times, have reached to God for miracles. Our needs have been great, and we have pleaded with Him to come to our aid. The scriptures, as well as our own history, teach us that the way He most often responds is through His faithful children who love their neighbors. This is where the gifts of the Spirit come in. When we need a gift, God inspires another loving soul to reach out and provide that gift. In doing so, His needy child receives the blessing. At the same time, another blessing flows, for the person who responded is also blessed. In this way, God can bless two, not just one. Such is the economy of heaven.

My point is that we are God's hands and feet and eyes and ears. He works through us. We are not ancillary or adjunct in His work; we are the heart and soul of it. We are immediate to our neighbor and, therefore, can be first in line to give service. Of course, we cannot be all things to all people. I really appreciate some counsel Elder Maxwell gave: "I have on my office wall a wise and useful reminder by Anne Morrow Lindbergh concerning one of the realities of life. She wrote, 'My life cannot implement in action the demands of all the people to whom my heart responds.' That's good counsel for us all, not as an excuse to forgo duty, but as a sage point about pace and the need for quality in relationships."[12] We must do all we can, but only as much as we can. God deliberately gives each of us only a few gifts by which we can bless. He does not expect us to be all things to all people. He does expect us to combine our talents with those of the community of believers, and in that way make a full contingent of gifts available for that community.

ON TOUGH LOVE

Another lesson we can learn from the story of the rich young ruler is that love has its tough side. The Savior brought the rich young ruler to self-realization because of His love for Him. It was the Savior's love that allowed the young man a choice. That is what real love is: tough, because it demands the very best of others; and realistic, because it demands only what they can give. When the very best is not given to God, no reward follows; salvation is forfeited. Love guarantees that God is no respecter of persons. All will face Him on the plain of His love. That is what God's judgment is all about. The Book of Mormon shows us that God's universe is one in which debt must be paid. God's love does not mean a people can sin with impunity, or that He will protect them from the consequences of sin. The Old Testament serves as a witness: Hosea insisted that if Judah sows the wind she will reap the whirlwind (Hosea 8:7), but God still loves Judah. That is the whole point. Her punishment, as it were, is not an indication that she is not loved. God loves her without measure. In fact, He calls her His bride, but He will not tolerate adultery without recompense.

The Hebrew verb for *love* and its cognate noun denote love freely given, a love coming from what God is toward those who are His.[13] This love is not irresistibly drawn from Him by persons of unusual virtue, but is freely given, even to sinners. The Old Testament underscores the unworthiness of many of those whom God loves as a means of highlighting the purity of that love. Therefore, as Leon Morris has said, "The constancy of His love depends on what He is rather than what we are."[14]

One thing we must get clear, however, is that sinning against God's love brings consequences. Seen in this light, unconditional love does not really exist. It is true that God will never cease loving us, but it is certainly wrong to think that his love will allow mercy to rob justice. No, His love assures us that justice will have its day. God hates sin, and those tainted with it will find that they come under the full measure of His censure. Paul understood this and explained it to some of his Hebrew brothers. They were having a hard time understanding why the Lord would chasten the sinner. Paul declared, "Ye have forgotten the exhortation which speaketh unto you as unto children." He then quotes that admonition found in Proverbs 3:11–12 (as found in the Septuagint). "My son, despise not thou the chastening of the Lord, nor faint when thou art rebuked of him: For whom the Lord loveth he chasteneth, and scourgeth every son whom he receiveth." Paul then concludes, "If ye endure chastening, God dealeth with you as with sons; for what son is he whom the father chasteneth not?" (Heb. 12:5–7). The point is that God's love is at the center of His rebuke, not peripheral to it. In other words, we should not set God's rebuke against His love, but should see it as a response of that love. God's love is not soft or indulgent; neither is His rebuke an expression of despair, nor even a display of temper.[15]

In God, we meet love in its purest form. We must not confuse such love with sentimentality. Sentimentality takes the easy way out, refusing firm action, or doing the distasteful, or looking at the long-term good. In the process, it leaves the loved one uncorrected in his sin, thus reinforcing the very flaw that true love should try to eradicate.[1]

The scriptures fully reveal the stern side of love. God's love will not let the sinner off free. God has so ordered the universe that eventually and invariably sin will bring its own punishment. We need only look at the Bible and Book of Mormon to see historical confirmation that it operates not just on individuals but among whole peoples. That does not mean God is vindictive, just waiting for people to sin so He can pounce. His love is everlasting and boundless. The Old Testament stresses the unending and undiminishing nature of God's love as He constantly works with His people to try to bring them to Him. In Hosea, He affirmed that Israel had gone after false gods and, as a consequence, "thou hast destroyed thyself; but in me is thine help" (Hosea 13:9). He promised, "I will heal their backsliding, I will love them freely: for mine anger is turned away from him" (Hosea 14:4). Punishment is only one of the ways in which He expresses that love. Consider how He is working in these latter days. He has said,

> How oft have I called upon you by the mouth of my servants, and by the ministering of angels, and by mine own voice, and by the voice of thunderings, and by the voice of lightnings, and by the voice of tempests, and by the voice of earthquakes, and great hailstorms, and by the voice of famines and pestilences of every kind, and by the great sound of a trump, and by the voice of judgment, and by the voice of mercy all the day long, and by the voice of glory and honor and the riches of eternal life, and would have saved you with an everlasting salvation, but ye would not! (D&C 43:25).

All these—the mercy, the pleading, the promise of glory, the angels, the tempests, the plagues, the pestilence—are equally a sign of God's eternal and never-decreasing love for His children. It operates independent of the merits of His people, and no amount of sin and rebellion or goodness and faith can diminish or add to it in any way.[17] God responds to their need for salvation and He works in whatever way will best bring His children to it. Therefore, His love does obligate His children. Though it is not dependent on their conduct, it expects good conduct as a response.

To emphasize, God's love is not conditional. Still, He loves certain virtues and expects them from His people. One of these is righteousness. Psalms 11:7 stresses this, saying (and here I translate from the Hebrew), "Jehovah is righteous, he loves righteous deeds, [and] the upright behold his face."[18] Though this verse conveys a precious truth, it also contains a grave warning. A righteous God expects righteousness in His followers. When one refuses righteousness, that person places himself not outside the bounds of God's love, but outside the scope of His blessing.[19]

A GOD OF JEALOUSY

There is reason for this. Ours is a God of passions. One passion we often overlook is jealousy.[20] Consider the Lord's statement in Exodus 34:14: " For thou shalt worship no other god: for the Lord, whose name is Jealous, is a jealous God."[21] The Hebrew word conveys the idea of intense emotion and can be translated as strong ardor or fervent zeal, as well as ardent jealousy. It identifies that feeling aroused when a cherished object or relationship is threatened. The Bible uses the word in a very positive sense. Still, the scripture shows it to be two-edged. On the one hand, jealousy causes God to cherish and protect even to bloodshed when necessary. On the other, it forms the basis of His demand for repentance or retribution when He is offended.

That God associates such intense emotion with Himself should stand as a warning, especially in the context where God first applied it to Himself. Israel was about to enter the promised land. They were going to possess lands, vineyards, cities, and wealth they did not develop. These were gifts from God. But He warned them that they had better not forget Him and seek other means to success, security, and further riches. Their temptation, He cautioned, would lie in going after other gods. If they were faithful to Him, His jealousy would act as their guard and champion. Conversely, if they rebelled against Him, they would provoke His jealousy to wrath against themselves. Israel could receive God's help only on condition of keeping His law. There is a good reason why. Consider the following idea:

> The fact that jealousy is associated repeatedly with the law, and invoked by God in the giving of the law, is of cardinal importance in understanding the law. The law of God is not a blind, impersonal, and mechanically operative force. It is neither Karma nor fate. The law of God is the law of the absolute and totally personal Creator whose law operates within the context of His love and hate, His grace towards His people and His wrath towards His enemies.[22]

Law does not work like electricity which flows whenever physical conditions for it are right. Electricity is impersonal, not caring what it does or how it helps or who it hurts. It reacts solely to its environment. That is not the case with divine law. It expresses God's love and power, and responds strictly thereto. It is totally personal.

> God restrains His wrath in patience and grace, or He destroys His enemies with an over-running flood of judgment (Nahum 1:8). From a humanistic and impersonalistic perspective, both the mercy of God to Assyria (Jonah 3:1-4:3) and the judgment of God on Assyria (Nahum 1:1-3:19) seem disproportionate, because an impersonal law is also an external law: it know only actions, not the heart. Man, as he applies the law of God, must judge the actions of man, but God, being absolute, judges the total man with total judgment. The jealousy of God is therefore the certain assurance of the infallibility of God's court of law. The evil which so easily escapes the courts of state cannot escape the judgment of God, which, both in time as well as beyond time, moves in terms of the total requirements of His law. The jealousy of God is the guarantee of justice.[23]

The scriptures clearly reveal the self-destructive nature of wickedness, but even here we see the hand of God operating. God does not allow "self-destruction to act as an impersonal nemesis, an independent self-operating moral law sweeping away all in its path. To do so would allow the powers of evil to carry all the inhabitants of the earth down with them to utter ruin."[24] The book of Revelation emphasizes that

God operates to control the direction, force, and extent of destruction. Nothing goes beyond the limits He sets[25]. And none escape it, for good or ill.

The Lord's judgment always operates. When we love one another it blesses us. When we do not, it allows us to destroy ourselves. Indeed, the Lord has prophesied that the great destructions in the last days will result when many of His children cease to love. He even tells us why love will die—"because iniquity shall abound, the love of men shall wax cold" (JS–M 1:30). Thus, the ability of people to love—whether it is love of God, of life, or of others—cools, then disappears in the frigid climate of iniquity.[26]

WHEN LOVE WAXES COLD

When love, the thermometer of righteousness, waxes cold enough, society dies. In Peter and Paul's day, it was the Church that succumbed to spiritual hypothermia. In our day, it will be the world. Iniquity grows from selfishness, and selfishness, as much as hate, stands as an antonym of love. Selfish people desire to please only themselves. What little love they have for others often dies when others' needs interfere with their wants. Selfishness is a kind of cement which hardens the heart, and that hard-heartedness brings disastrous results. Such people think nothing of breaking covenants in order to fulfill desire.[27] They care little for the suffering of others, even when they cause it.[28]

Callousness has additional effect. As the Lord told Enoch of the iniquitous people in his day, "my fierce anger is kindled against them; for their hearts have waxed hard, and their ears are dull of hearing, and their eyes cannot see afar off" (Moses 6:27). Selfishness and iniquity cause society to become deaf and blind to its own predicament. This was the very condition which contributed to the great flood. The Savior noted that conditions in the last days will mirror those of the days of Noah, "for it shall be with them, as it was in the days which were before the flood; for until the day that Noah entered into the ark they were eating and drinking, marrying and giving in marriage; And knew not until the flood came, and took them all away; so shall also the coming of the Son of Man be " (JS–M

1:42–43). There are two important points here. First, in spite of the warnings of God and His prophets, the people insisted on perpetuating their kind of society by eating, drinking, and marrying. There was no repentance, no remorse, no sensitivity that any change was necessary, even though "the earth was corrupt before God, and it was filled with violence" (Moses 8:28). Second, they were blind to the fact that God would not allow the conditions they created to continue. Warning after warning came and sign after sign was given, yet the people could neither hear nor see due to the malaise of iniquity.

Do not get the feeling, however, that these people knew happiness. Lovelessness sees no purpose or meaning to life. As a result, "despair replaces joy. Anomie or drift drive out purpose. When people mock God's messengers and despise His words, deterioration sets in 'till there [is] no remedy' (see 2 Chr. 36:16)."[29]

People feel the illness, but refuse to see and apply the cure. Dissonance results, which expresses itself as a kind of existential nihilism. That, in turn, breeds fear—another antonym of love. Thus, the less love there is in a society, the more fear.[30] People dare not go out, especially at night—in some areas, people become prisoners in their own houses.

It is interesting that when love waxes cold, joy disappears. Not only that, but its sister, happiness, and its weak cousin, pleasure, also depart. People end up enjoying nothing. When they seek sweet gratification outside God's rules, they end up with bitter dust. Consider those iniquitous Nephites living near the end of their civilization. Of them Mormon reports that "they did curse God, and wish to die. Nevertheless they would struggle with the sword for their lives" (Morm. 2:14). Hatred for life, fear of death. No joy. No happiness. No pleasure. Just unremitting hate and never-ending fear.

THE NEED FOR FAITH, HOPE, AND CHARITY

Our task is to stop, or at least impede, the coming of this living hell on earth. And we can. John articulated the remedy: "There is no fear in love; but perfect love casteth out fear: because fear hath torment. He that feareth is not made perfect in love" (1 Jn 4:18). Elder Maxwell counseled:

> Events can shake us, bring on despair, and cause us to
> shrivel up in our capacity to love—unless we have *faith and
> love* based on truths that are relevant not only now but in
> eternity! We may become bearers not only of revealed
> truths—but of that precious needed commodity, hope,
> which significantly is part of that triad of truths—faith,
> hope and charity—without which nothing else is really
> relevant![31]

Faith, hope, and charity are the keys to latter-day survival. It is not
hard to see why. By these three we strive to keep God's commandments. Indeed, love especially leads to obedience—to service. When
we love, we respond to the needs and desires of others, including God.
We show the depth of our love for the Father to the degree we strive to
keep His commandments. Both the Old and New Testaments link the
two. In the second commandment, God expresses favor for "them that
love me, and keep my commandments" (Ex. 20:6). The Savior said it
even more bluntly: "If ye love me, keep my commandments" (John
14:15). Love and obedience are identical twins. Moses stressed the
need for his people to not only accept God's love, but to actively
return it: "Know therefore that the Lord thy God, he is God, the
faithful God, which keepeth covenant and mercy with them that love
him and keep his commandments to a thousand generations" (Deut.
7:9). The prophet promised Israel that, in return for their love,
Jehovah "will love thee, and bless thee, and multiply thee: he will also
bless the fruit of thy womb, and the fruit of thy land, thy corn, and
thy wine, and thine oil, the increase of thy kine, and the flocks of thy
sheep, in the land which he sware unto thy fathers to give thee" (Deut.
7:13). Israel's distinctive view of both God and man rests in the
mutual and reciprocal affection that each can have for the other.[32]

HOW LOVE FULFILLS THE LAW AND THE PROPHETS

Thus, we see that love forms the foundation of man's relationship
with God and God's with man. Therefore, the love commandment
stands as center of the whole gospel program. Matthew records the
Savior's teaching that "thou shalt love the Lord thy God with all thy

heart, and with all thy soul, and with all thy mind. This is the first
and great commandment. And the second is like unto it, Thou shalt
love thy neighbor as thyself (Matt. 23:37–39). Notice two items especially. First, the second commandment is "like unto" the first. The
idea in the Greek is that the two cannot be separated into first-place
and second-place commandments. Rather, the two should be taken as
one command, each part equally important with the other. Second,
the Jews used the term "the law and the prophets" to identify the
whole of the Bible, "the law" meaning the first five books, and "the
prophets" meaning the latter portion, thus including all the contents
of the Bible. Thus, this single commandment with its dual components summarizes the whole biblical code.

To see how this one commandment fulfills the whole law,
consider Paul's beautiful testimony in 1 Corinthians 13. We will
begin by looking at verses 1–3.

> Though I speak with the tongues of men and of angels,
> and have not charity, I am become as sounding brass, or a
> tinkling cymbal. And though I have the gift of prophecy,
> and understand all mysteries, and all knowledge; and
> though I have all faith, so that I could remove mountains,
> and have not charity, I am nothing. And though I bestow
> all my goods to feed the poor, and though I give my body
> to be burned, and have not charity, it profiteth me
> nothing.

The Apostle begins by emphasizing that love is the greatest of the
gifts of God and goes on to show its importance. The King James
Bible translates "love" as "charity" throughout Paul's writings here.[33]
Paul's point is that love gives value to all our actions. It allows us to
do the right thing for the right reason. Paul continues, in verses 4–7,
to list the qualities associated with love:

> Charity suffereth long, and is kind; charity envieth not;
> charity vaunteth not itself, is not puffed up, Doth not
> behave itself unseemly, seeketh not her own, is not easily
> provoked, thinketh no evil; Rejoiceth not in iniquity, but

rejoiceth in the truth; Beareth all things, believeth all
things, hopeth all things, endureth all things.

Note the point he makes: love is not simply a way of feeling, but a
way of expressing that feeling. Those who possess these qualities really
do love. They do not simply profess love. Thus, the list becomes a
kind of litmus test to see if we possess or merely profess love.[34]

Paul's words bear careful study. He says, "Charity suffereth long."
The Greek word expresses patience, a willingness to allow God time
to do His work while remaining faithful, and it also connotes that
courtesy shown to others while they mature spiritually.[35] Paul goes on
to say that love "is kind." His word denotes a basic goodness which
expresses itself in being kind toward others.[36] Paul knows that "charity
envieth not." This attribute emphasizes the generous nature of love.
Paul castigates jealousy or envy of another's good fortune.[37] The next
virtue Paul lists is the flip side of the one above. He says, "charity
vaunteth not itself." His word condemns the braggart.[38] Paul shows
that true love is modest. It does not boast or put on airs. Indeed, it "is
not puffed up." The King James text translates Paul's word literally.[39]
Being "puffed up" discloses a prideful attitude. Love cannot keep
company with conceit. Its basic humility keeps it from being snob-
bish or feeling superior to others. Love "doth not behave itself
unseemly." Paul's word describes disgraceful or rude acts; love shows
respect and courtesy at all times.[40] Next, Paul says that love "seeketh
not her own." His phrase means that love is not concerned with its
own interests.[41] It is not self-seeking or selfish. It willingly gives to
others as it can. Further, it "is not easily provoked." The Greek word
mentioned here comes from the idea of being sharp and suggests
general irritability.[42] Love is even tempered. It is not prone to anger,
nor is it quick to take offense. Again, love "thinketh no evil." Paul's
word means to note or count up and carries the idea of reckoning
offenses.[43] Love is forgiving. It neither keeps score nor broods over
past injuries. Finally, Paul says that love "rejoiceth not in iniquity, but
rejoiceth in the truth." Iniquity here means injustice, bad deeds done
by and to oneself.[44] Love does not gloat over the sins of others, nor
does it care for that which is wrong. It is constructive, helpful, and
effectual. Paul summarizes by saying that love "beareth all things,

believeth all things, hopeth all things, endureth all things." Love submits to God and His rule. It keeps faith through hope, remaining ever constant in the things of God.

Therefore, Paul can say, "Charity never faileth: but whether there be prophecies, they shall fail; whether there be tongues, they shall cease; whether there be knowledge, it shall vanish away" (v. 8). Paul highlights the enduring nature of love. Other divine gifts will eventually pass away. All prophecies will be fulfilled. Someday all will speak the pure tongue of God. Eventually our imperfect knowledge and wisdom will be supplanted by that which is perfect. Indeed, now "we know in part, and we prophesy in part. But when that which is perfect is come, then that which is in part shall be done away" (v. 9–10). Not so with love. Along with faith and hope, it remains the eternal constant.

Paul then gives sterling advice, saying, "When I was a child, I spake as a child, I understood as a child, I thought as a child: but when I became a man, I put away childish things" (v. 11). Here he is calling us to come to maturity through love. Selfishness, envy, strife, boasting, and so on, are part of immaturity and lovelessness. All these produce the spiritual blindness discussed above. It is noteworthy that without love, a person can hardly even see himself. Consider Paul's comment, "For now we see through a glass, darkly; but then face to face: now I know in part; but then shall I know even as also I am known" (v. 12). Now, without love, we peer into a looking glass, a small hand mirror (they were made of shiny bronze in Paul's day), trying to discover our true self. We cannot see because our loveless mirror is distorted, scarred, perhaps cracked, and much too small. But then, when we are filled with love, we shall truly see and understand who and what we really are. Without love we know ourselves only partially, but when filled with God's love, we shall know ourselves as well as God knows us. John understood that "when he shall appear, we shall be like him; for we shall see him as he is" (1 Jn. 3:2). He is love and we will be love as well.

Paul concludes his study on love, saying, "And now abideth faith, hope, charity, these three; but the greatest of these is charity" (v. 13).

THE WHOLE LAW OF GOD IS LOVE

Paul's discussion helps us understand why the commandment to love contains all the law and the prophets. Those who are immature need the Ten Commandments because they must be told exactly how to behave. Paul described the law as "our schoolmaster to bring us unto Christ, that we might be justified by faith. But after that faith is come, we are no longer under a schoolmaster. For ye are all the children of God by faith in Christ Jesus" (Gal. 3:24–26). The language of the King James text may mislead us a bit. Paul does not have in mind an actual school teacher.[45] The more wealthy Roman households appointed an educated slave to look after and teach the sons of the house proper social behavior.[46] The primary job of these slaves (think of them in terms of a nanny) was not to teach reading or writing, but "to mold the breed." Until the youth came of age, he was totally under the power of the slave who taught him proper public grace. Once the child matured, he became master over the "nanny" and was subservient only to his father.

Paul here teaches us that God designed the law to be a "nanny," to hold the immature in check and teach them proper behavior toward Him and one another. He understood the law in the same terms as Abinadi, who explained that:

> [I]t was expedient that there should be a law given to the children of Israel, yea, even a very strict law; for they were a stiffnecked people, quick to do iniquity, and slow to remember the Lord their God; Therefore there was a law given them, yea, a law of performances and of ordinances, a law which they were to observe strictly from day to day, to keep them in remembrance of God and their duty towards him (Mosiah 13:29–30).

Those who are mature are freed from this multitude of performances and ordinances. One who loves God automatically worships only Him and keeps the Sabbath day holy; he does not need to be told to do so. One who loves wife or husband finds the very thought of adultery abhorrent. One who loves neighbor as self never steals, or lies, or cheats, or kills. It simply would not be in him and, therefore, no one would need to tell him not to do these things.

Therefore, the mature only need one commandment: thou shalt love. They do not have to worry about all the minuscule statutes and decrees within the law; they do not have to concern themselves over ritual cleanliness or uncleanliness; they are beyond all daily offerings and observances. Love makes them free of the law of Moses. No wonder Paul saw in love perfect freedom and the vision by which we come to know both God and ourselves.

LOVE AS THE SOLE POWER OF THE UNIVERSE

Love, however, is not only the power by which we know God and ourselves; it describes the very essence of the power of the universe. Some may say that the seat of all power is faith, for by it God made the worlds and by faith all miracles are performed. But Paul understood that "faith . . . worketh by love" (Gal. 5:6). We have already learned that love gives value to all the other gifts of the Spirit. That includes faith. Therefore, even the power of faith draws its force, direction, and purpose from love.

This gives us a real understanding of the nature of God's omnipotence. One hundred and one times the scriptures refer to Him as the "Almighty." How is He the Almighty? It is because He has forged the greatest fetter by which He has cuffed and controls the cosmos. He has woven the strongest cable, from the coils of which nothing can get away. He has linked together the strongest chain and bound all by it. And what is that fetter, cable, and chain? When I was young and seeing through the eyes of the immature, I believed that God was omnipotent because he alone possessed the full power of unlimited coercion. Like the mythical Thor, He owned, as it were, the hammer which could destroy us all. Therefore, He brought the cosmos to heel by spreading fear bordering on terror. My poor misguided understanding had led me far from the truth. History itself should have taught me how ephemeral terror and fear are in binding people under a despot's rule. Eventually, desire for freedom and respite overcome fear and destroy the terror.

The power by which God binds has nothing to do with fear, for there is no fear in love. And there we come to the heart of it. God created the cosmos, and the cosmos is good. Take this earth for example. God created a cognizant, living entity that is well aware of her existence and all that happens upon her. Through divine power, the prophet Enoch was able to understand the cry of the earth as she mourned, "Wo, wo is me, the mother of men; I am pained, I am weary, because of the wickedness of my children. When shall I rest, and be cleansed from the filthiness which is gone forth out of me? When will my Creator sanctify me, that I may rest, and righteousness for a season abide upon my face?" (Moses 7:48). And of her the Lord said, "The earth abideth the law of a celestial kingdom, for it filleth the measure of its creation, and transgresseth not the law— Wherefore, it shall be sanctified; yea, notwithstanding it shall die, it shall be quickened again, and shall abide the power by which it is quickened, and the righteous shall inherit it" (D&C 88:25–26). She is willfully obedient to her God. Helaman said, "O how great is the nothingness of the children of men; yea, even they are less than the dust of the earth. For behold, the dust of the earth moveth hither and thither, to the dividing asunder, at the command of our great and everlasting God" (Helaman 12:7–8). The earth obeys her God instantly and without question. Why? Because she deeply loves her Creator and her Lord. Whatever He commands, she does.

That is not only true of the earth but of the cosmos as well. God has bound all to Him through the cuffs of His self-sacrificing love. No chain or cable or fetters could be stronger. That means God does not have to coerce, nor does anyone who loves and is loved in return. Thus, the scripture promises:

> Let thy bowels also be full of charity towards all men, and to the household of faith, and let virtue garnish thy thoughts unceasingly; then shall thy confidence wax strong in the presence of God; and the doctrine of the priesthood shall distill upon thy soul as the dews from heaven. The Holy Ghost shall be thy constant companion, and thy scepter an unchanging scepter of righteousness and truth; and thy dominion shall be an everlasting dominion, and without compulsory means it shall flow unto thee forever and ever (D&C 121:45–46).

"Without compulsory means." That is how it works. There is no compulsion in love. Only persuasion. Therefore, God is Almighty because He has all love. And those virtuous souls who love and serve fully shall also become omnipotent.

CONCLUSION

No wonder the tree which Lehi saw was so beautiful! It represented the key to safety and of salvation here on earth, of eternal life in the world to come, and of true omnipotence and the fulness of joy. And little wonder the Savior said that the great commandment was to love God and neighbor. With love, every good thing is bound together in one. Out of this grows perfect freedom. Paul said it best: "Brethren, ye have been called unto liberty; . . . [therefore] by love serve one another, For all the law is fulfilled in one word, even in this; Thou shalt love thy neighbour as thyself" (Gal. 5:13–14).

CHAPTER 8
OVERCOMING *the* IMPEDIMENTS
to LOVE *and* JOY

The beautiful tree in Lehi's vision contained the key to obtaining "exeedingly great joy" (1 Ne. 8:12), and not surprisingly, its beauty beckoned to many. Lehi saw "numberless concourses of people, many of whom were pressing forward, that they might obtain the path which led unto the tree" (1 Ne. 8:21). Some realized their goal and actually commenced "in the path" (v. 22). Most of the people he saw, however, did not even try. Among those who did, many were not able to stay the course. A number of impediments arose that distracted the people from achieving joy. The two biggest, Nephi learned, were the temptations of the devil and the pride of the world.

The Lord symbolized satanic temptations as "mists of darkness" which arose to obscure the path. Nephi's guiding angel explained that these mists "blindeth the eyes, and hardeneth the hearts of the children of men, and leadeth them away into broad roads, that they perish and are lost" (1 Ne. 12:17). Caving in to temptation blinds the eyes toward truth as it hardens the heart toward others. Acute selfishness sets in, making it easy for the devil to lead people onto the broad path of self-destruction.

The message of the vision is clear: humankind cannot create its own way to love and joy. If we are to achieve both, we must follow the path God has set: it alone can get us past the blinding and hardening effects of Satan's temptations. Yet, recognizing the path, and even starting on it, is not good enough. We must go all the way to the tree. Of course, Satan is always straining to seduce people off the straight and narrow and onto the broad way. The philosophies of men and of demons are very seductive. They are able to mask lies and make dark appear as light.

Lehi saw that there was only one way through the mists to the tree. "I beheld a rod of iron, and it extended along the bank of the river, and led to the tree by which I stood" (1 Ne. 8:19). He saw many "pressing forward, and they came forth and caught hold of the end of the rod of iron; and they did press forward through the mist of darkness, clinging to the rod of iron, even until they did come forth and partake of the fruit of the tree" (1 Ne. 8:24). Here God, via Nephi, revealed the means of escaping Satan's ploys: "I beheld that the rod of iron, which my father had seen, was the word of God" (1 Ne. 11:25). Throughout time, the Lord reveals His mysteries and His will through His prophets (see Amos 3:7). Their teachings, whether written or oral, constitute the word of God, outlining the path to joy. We cannot ignore, trivialize, or take casually the prophets' counsel. Those who do so will fail to grasp the rod, and will not achieve love or joy. In the first chapter of this study we read President Benson's promise that "the gospel principles are the steps and guidelines which will help us find true happiness and joy."[1] To use Lehi's analogy, the iron rod—God's commandments—marks the straight and narrow way to love, keeping on the path until we obtain a fulness of joy.

But even getting to the tree, as we discovered in chapter five, does not assure us of eternal life and love. Lehi saw many who "did press their way forward, continually holding fast to the rod of iron, until they came forth and fell down and partook of the fruit of the tree" (1 Ne. 8:30). To his dismay, he also saw many who did not remain true: "After they had tasted of the fruit they were ashamed, . . . and they fell away into forbidden paths and were lost" (1 Ne. 8:28). What would cause them to leave the tree of love? That question brings us to the second impediment to love and joy that Lehi saw.

Many, he tells us, were attracted to a great and spacious building, which beckoned with seductive allure. Lehi saw that it "was filled with people, both old and young, both male and female; and their manner of dress was exceedingly fine; and they were in the attitude of mocking and pointing their fingers towards those who had come to the tree and were partaking of the fruit" (1 Ne. 8:27). Nephi's guide explained, as we learned in chapter five, that "the great and spacious building was the pride of the world" (1 Ne. 11:36). Sadly, many of those who had already partaken of God's love, could not ignore the mocking scorn of the world. They became ashamed of their love and fell away.

As we learned in chapter one, John the Revelator understood that "the fearful, and unbelieving," that is, the cowards and the faithless, "shall have their part in the lake which burneth with fire and brimstone" (Rev. 21:8). John, like Nephi, looked to the last days when the great and spacious building would be strong and its inhabitants particularly adept at pointing "the finger of scorn" (1 Ne. 8:33). He knew that their objective would be to cause those who love God to turn away from Him in shame. Under the unremitting pressure of the pride of the world, courage and faithfulness become supreme virtues, cowardice and unfaithfulness great sins. Those who experience the sweet love of God and then turn away fall "into forbidden paths" (1 Ne. 8:28) where the power of the second death awaits.[2]

Paul understood that the world will always try to shame the believer. While in Athens, he was called a babbler and "a setter forth of strange gods" (Acts 17:18; see v. 32). Courageously, he proclaimed that "I am not ashamed of the gospel of Christ: for it is the power of God unto salvation to every one that believeth; to the Jew first, and also to the Greek" (Rom. 1:16). By rejecting the shame of the world, Paul won the accolades of God. Jacob, the son of Lehi, testified to his people that "they who have believed in the Holy One of Israel, they who have endured the crosses of the world, and despised the shame of it, they shall inherit the kingdom of God, which was prepared for them from the foundation of the world, and their joy shall be full forever" (2 Ne. 9:18). Facing the crosses made by those in the great and spacious building takes tremendous courage, but it brings salvation. Many, unfortunately, will trade the kingdom of God for the great and spacious building, and the fulness of heavenly joy for a brief flash of the world's acceptance.

While partaking of God's love is no assurance that we will stay true, there is something that will help. Lehi tells us how he and others did it. He admits he saw the derision. Those in the great building "did point the finger of scorn at me and those that were partaking of the fruit also; but we heeded them not" (1 Ne. 8:33). There is the key—the faithful gave no heed; they ignored the rejection and disgrace of the world. To heed means "to pay attention to" due to fear, want, interest, or intrigue. Those who successfully remained with Lehi at the tree did so because they neither feared the world nor found interest in what it had to offer. Thus, they entered into a fullness of joy.

THE FEAR OF JOY

Remember also that many people in Lehi's vision not only turned their back on joy, but also mocked those who would not do the same. This seems to have been the largest camp. At first that surprised me, but when I really thought about it, I came to see the truth of it. Hugh Nibley asked a very apt question that comes into play as we end our study. "What are we afraid of?" he enquires.

> What do men fear most? Believe it or not, it is joy. Against joy, society erects its most massive bulwarks. The gospel is a message of terrifying joy. What is the culmination of all joy? To stand in the presence of God and behold his face—we don't need to argue that point. Yet what is the most frightening prospect that mortal man can imagine? Certainly, to stand in the presence of God and behold his face! The presence of Jesus was an unbearable torment to wicked men and devils alike; rather than look upon the face of the Lord, the wicked shall beg the rocks and the mountains to cover them; the Apostles who cheerfully faced death at the hands of devilish men were "sore afraid" at the approach of God the Father on the mountain; and when Moses descended from another mountain, the people fell down in deadly fear at the presence of one who had been talking face to face with God, though Moses himself at an earlier time had "hid his face; for he was afraid to look upon God" (Ex. 3:6). It is not hell that men fear most, but heaven. Plainly the joy for which man was created is no light and trivial thing.[3]

The task that lies ahead for those of us who seek exaltation is overcoming our fear of joy, and breaking down the barriers we set up against it. How does God get us past our self-erected bulwarks? It is only through love. Love's flames can burn all gates and stockades; its battering rams can breach all walls. We must, however, allow it to touch our defenses. The result is wonderful; we become like God, for we are one with Him. We will never be free of love's power again. As Paul affirmed, "I am persuaded, that neither death, nor life, nor angels, nor principalities, nor powers, nor things present, nor things to come, Nor height, nor depth, nor any other creature, shall be able to separate us from the love of God, which is in Christ Jesus our Lord" (Rom. 8:38–39). The Saint stands always within the love of God; joy results.

Joy is what we receive when we play by the rules of love. These rules are strange rules from the world's standpoint, but they do work. As Edwin Markham so clearly expressed it:

He drew a circle that shut me out—
Heretic, rebel, a thing to flout.
But love and I had the wit to win:
We drew a circle that took him in.[4]

The world cannot understand such behavior, and since it has long since shut its gates against joy, it will, unfortunately, never understand. We, however, can still see how it works. When we accept God's love, our ability to love increases and our desire to serve does as well. Our circle of love ever widens to bring us to that joy which surpasses understanding.

That is how God destroys the bulwarks against joy. He distracts us, helping us forget our fear of joy, by calling us to selflessly serve. Yielding to His call causes us to care for others, putting them before ourselves. That, in the end, is what will bring us to joy. A conversation I overheard between two boys in one of my seminary classes long ago illustrates the point. It seems that on their way to seminary, which was held in a home near the high school, the boys had stopped for a moment to assist a neighbor woman rake her lawn. She suffered from cataracts, making it very hard for her to see details and, apparently, she was doing a poor job of cleaning up. Both boys quickly straightened the area. She was delighted with the help and offered each boy an apple, which they graciously accepted. They were still eating the apples as they entered the house where I taught. As they waited for other students to arrive, one commented to the other that he thought his apple was the sweetest he had ever tasted. "Only thing sweeter," said his friend, "was the look in that lady's eyes." I inquired what he meant and they told me what had happened and how it made them feel. These boys had found joy. That's what made their apples seem sweeter; they were sugared with service.

JOY, A BY-PRODUCT OF SERVICE

It is most interesting that they found joy without seeking it. In fact, had they set out for joy, they may have missed it altogether. Consider a thought of a mentor of mine, Arthur Henry King:

> One of the mistakes we make over and over again in life is to go directly for the things we think are important. But if we aim at self-fulfillment, we shall never be fulfilled. If we aim at education, we shall never become educated. If we aim at salvation, we shall never be saved. These things are indirect, supreme results of doing something else; and the something else is service, it is righteousness, it is trying to do the right thing, the thing that needs to be done at each moment.[5]

Selfishness leads neither to love nor joy. But loving service, conscious only of what needs to be done at the moment, leads to both.

The circle of our love will not initially be all embracing, nor is it necessary that it be so; it grows as we practice service. Even the Savior, as we learned in chapter two, "received not of the fulness at first, but received grace for grace" and "continued from grace to grace, until he received a fulness" (D&C 93:12–13). All must grow toward a fulness of light, truth, love, and joy through service. At the outset, God's grace is there to aid us. Our job is to accept and magnify His grace.

THE MEANING OF LIFE

And so we return to the beginning, looking again at my son's question. Does life have meaning? Is there purpose to existence? The scriptures chorus a rousing "yes!" Adam deliberately brought about the existence of humankind. In doing so, he gave all of us a shot at achieving a fulness of joy. God designed the plan of salvation to that end, and no other end. The way He authored for His children to obtain that fulness was through love and the service that it generates.

This idea explains not only the purpose of existence but also why God does what He does. To Moses, He revealed that His work and glory consists of bringing about the immortality and exaltation of his children (see Moses 1:39), which is to bequeath eternal joy. Some, who have never really understood the power of love, have speculated that God must reside in a state of eternal and extreme boredom, being boxed into an endless repetition of creation. They fear that there is never anything new to grab the attention or hold the interest of the Omniscient. Elder Maxwell warned that "those who try to qualify God's omniscience fail to understand that He has no need to avoid ennui by learning new things. Because God's love is also perfect, there is, in fact, divine delight in that 'one eternal round' which, to us, seems to be all routine and repetition. God derives His great and continuing joy and glory by increasing and advancing His creations, and not from new intellectual experiences."[6]

John defined the point where we join God in His work. The Apostle admonished, "Beloved, let us love one another: for love is of God; and every one that loveth is born of God, and knoweth God" (1 Jn. 4:7). Note how John reiterates Peter; clearly, it is through loving each other that we come to fully know God. John goes on to testify that "if we love one another, God dwelleth in us, and his love is perfected in us. Hereby know we that we dwell in him, and he in us, because he hath given us of his Spirit" (1 Jn. 4:12–13). In other words, the Spirit combined with love, which is the token of the Spirit, become the signs that we are one with God. In loving one another, even if imperfectly, we grow toward perfection and greater love. With perfection comes the ability to love fully and purely.

So John continues, "Herein is our love made perfect, that we may have boldness in the day of judgment: because as he is, so are we in this world" (1 Jn. 4:17). Love has many objectives; one is to prepare us for judgment. The person who is full of love looks forward to Judgment Day. God, in the Doctrine and Covenants, gives us insight as to why: "Intelligence cleaveth unto intelligence; wisdom receiveth wisdom; truth embraceth truth; virtue loveth virtue; light cleaveth unto light" (D&C 88:40). In other words, values attract their like. Since God is love, those who have love will, with delight, be drawn to Him. There will not be fear of His judgment or of His joy, for these things will bring peace, unity, and eternal fellowship.

Having that Spirit in our lives allows us to live in the world as the Savior did, that is, by loving and serving. John knew the result: "These things write we unto you, that your joy may be full" (1 Jn 1:4). He understood that joy is coupled with, and dependent on, love. Joy results from accepting the gift of love God has given us in His Son, accepting the love-gift the Savior has given us in His Atonement, and accepting the responsibility to love as They have loved.

The Savior brought it all together with these words:

> As the Father hath loved me, so have I loved you: continue ye in my love. If ye keep my commandments, ye shall abide in my love; even as I have kept my Father's commandments, and abide in his love. These things have I spoken unto you, that my joy might remain in you, and that your joy might be full. This is my commandment, That ye love one another, as I have loved you (John 15:9–12).

CONCLUSION

Allow me to close our study with two experiences. A student came into my office one day after completing a service project sponsored by the Institute where I was teaching. He was filled with that satisfaction that comes with heartfelt and unselfish service. He told me he really enjoyed helping others. After I told him how much I appreciated his sacrifice, he assured me that it was no sacrifice. I then said, only half teasing, that his attitude would assure him additional blessings from heaven. He said he wished that were true, but because he had not sacrificed, no blessings would come. That made me curious and I asked him what he meant. He said that his father had taught his family that in order for sacrifice to be real—to be considered a sacrifice—it had to have an element of difficulty, of hardship, perhaps even of hurt. If it did not hurt, he emphasized, there was no sacrifice and, thus, no blessings.

Does sacrifice really have to hurt to be sanctifying? I hope that through our study, you can see the untruth in that statement. I will admit that without the fulness of love, much of what God asks us to do can be hard, challenging, uncomfortable, and perhaps even pinch a bit. Frankly, I still struggle with callings outside my comfort zone and requests for time or funds beyond what I have budgeted. I am sure that in the giving, I am blessed. Nevertheless, I have found over the years that as I have truly come to care for others, there is less and less that either discomforts or pinches. I am convinced that when I love God and my fellows enough, no sacrifice will be painful. There is no pain in loving service and love filled sacrifice, only joy. Getting there can be painful, but once we are there, the pain is gone.

When we come to love, then the greatest sacrifices are possible because there is no reserve, no holding back, no resentment, envy, grudging, annoyance, aggravation, or pain. Both service and sacrifice become a pleasure and a delight. God Himself has sacrificed for His children, even giving His Only Begotten Son, yet God gave Jesus through love, and, though He hated to see His Son hurt, there was no pain in the giving. We, too, must come to this point.

The second experience occurred some time ago as I was talking with a colleague, a well-respected man who had accumulated quite a number of awards and praises through years of service. He beamed as he shared with me an experience he had had the past weekend attending an awards ceremony. I could feel a delight and enthusiasm coming from him—a real sense of joy—that I had never seen before. What I found interesting was that he was not the one being honored; the focus was on his beloved wife, his companion of thirty-plus years. She was a kindly, dignified, reserved woman who felt most comfortable supporting and encouraging her husband, in giving him the confidence and energy to succeed. Over the years, she had received little recognition for all she had done. This night, however, she was presented with her stake's Exemplary Womanhood Award, complete with white roses and plaudits.

His eyes were moist, but his face beamed as he shared with me his joy that she had stood for a moment in the spotlight. That day, I saw eternity in his eyes. We had talked in times past after he had received awards, but never had I seen such radiance in him. I felt that no award he had ever received—no round of applause, no placard or trophy, no honorarium—brought him as much joy as the moment when others recognized and honored his wife.

So it is when we come to love—others' successes, others' conquests, others' triumphs become our own, and in that we find delight. Truly, Paul taught us the more excellent way. There will always be faith, hope, and charity, but the greatest of these is charity. And why? Because that is the way that God will bring us to eternal glory and a fulness of joy.

CHAPTER NOTES

Notes to Chapter One

1. Joseph Smith, *Teachings of the Prophet Joseph Smith* (Salt Lake City: Deseret Book, 1976), 255.

2. *Webster's New Dictionary of Synonyms* (Springfield, Mass. Merriam-Webster Inc., 1984), s.v. "happiness."

3. Admittedly, we must be careful not to place too much emphasis on the use of any particular word in the Book of Mormon. Unlike the Bible, we cannot check the original language to see just how broadly or narrowly a term could have been translated.

4. Smith, *Teachings*, 255.

5. *Synonyms*, s.v. "happiness."

6. Ibid., s.v. "joy."

7. Smith, *Teachings*, 295.

8. David O. McKay in *Gospel Ideals*, ed. G. Homer Durham (Salt Lake City: Deseret Sunday School Union Board, 1957), 491-92, noted the negative side of pleasure when he admonished the Saints, saying, "Let us in life distinguish between the joy that the Prophet Lehi had in mind when he said, 'men are, that they might have joy,' and the pleasure that the world is seeking by indulging in appetites and passions, vainly hoping to find happiness. Happiness springs from within. . . . Pleasure is not the purpose of man's existence. Joy is."

9. *Synonyms*, s.v. "happiness."

10. Ibid., s.v. "pleasure."

11. Ibid.

12. We have no way of knowing how long Adam and Eve were in the garden before they fell, but we must not assume that their stay was brief. In fact, they may have been there for an extended period. Consider what we know. Adam was placed on the earth on the sixth day (Moses 2:27–31). Then, "on the seventh day I, God, ended my work, and all things which I had made; and I rested on the seventh day from all my work, and all things which I had made were finished, and I, God, saw that they were good; And I, God, blessed the seventh day, and sanctified it; because that in it I had rested from all my work which I, God, had created and made" (Moses 3:2–3). Peter informs us that "one day is with the Lord as a thousand years, and a thousand years as one day" (2 Pet. 3:8). Expanding on this idea, the Pearl of Great Price teaches us that the time of "Kolob was after the manner of the Lord, according to its times and seasons in the revolutions thereof; that one revolution was a day unto the Lord, after his manner of reckoning, it being one thousand years according to the time appointed unto that whereon thou standest" (Abr. 3:4). Abraham then informs us that, in the garden, Adam's time "was after the Lord's time, which was after the time of Kolob; for as yet the Gods had not appointed unto Adam his reckoning" (Abr. 5:13). So Adam could have been in the garden a long time before he and Eve decided to fall "that men might be."

13. B. H. Roberts, *New Witnesses for God* (Salt Lake City: George Q. Cannon & Sons, 1895), 3:201.

14. B. H. Roberts, *The Gospel: An Exposition of Its First Principles and Man's Relationship to Deity*, 11th ed., (Salt Lake City: Deseret Book, 1966), 8.

15. The Greek *peirasmos* means "trial" or "difficulty." The sense of the Greek word includes trials, difficulties, or suffering which provide a means for strengthening the soul and making it fit for eternal life.

16. The Greek reads, in transliteration, *dè agalliâsthe charâ aneklal ēt ō kaí dedoksasménē*, "and rejoice with unutterable and exalted joy."

17. Neal A. Maxwell, *Even As I Am* (Salt Lake City: Deseret Book, 1982), 91.

18. Roberts, *New Witnesses*, 3:204.

19. Ibid.

20. My approach with the class was a bit dramatic. Nonetheless, though none of the "third part" were really destroyed so far as their identity was concerned, the family relationship with the Father was indeed destroyed forever.

21. Neal A. Maxwell, *All These Things Shall Give Thee Experience* (Salt Lake City: Deseret Book, 1979), 15.

22. Neal A. Maxwell, *Deposition of a Disciple* (Salt Lake City: Deseret Book, 1976), 28.

23. Neal A. Maxwell, *Even As I Am* , 34.

24. Smith, *Teachings*, 255-56.

25. Brigham Young, *Discourses of Brigham Young*, ed. John A. Widtsoe (Salt Lake City: Deseret Book, 1975), 428.

26. The Hebrew root (*štn*), from which the noun Satan is derived, carries the idea of accusing, attacking, or bringing into bad light. The verb form denotes any adversarial relationship. The noun form of the word (Hebrew *sâtân* or Greek *satanās*) described an adversary, one who wilfully opposes or attacks another.

27. Greek word is *paráklētos.*

28. The Greek *paraklēsis* denotes a summons, entreaty, or call for assistance.

29. Apparently, Satan led Cain to believe that Cain's acts could be hidden from God. Note Cain's surprised reaction, in Moses 5:39, to the Lord's knowledge of Abel's murder.

30. With insight, C. S. Lewis had a devil, Screwtape, contrast the aims of the Savior and of Satan. Said Screwtape, "God really *does* want to fill the universe with a lot of loathsome little replicas of Himself—creatures whose life, on its miniature scale, will be qualitatively like His own, not because he has absorbed them but because their wills freely conform to His. We want cattle who can finally become food; he wants servants who can finally become sons. . . . We are empty and would be filled; he is full and flows over. Our war aim is a world in which Our Father Below has drawn all other beings into himself" *(The Screwtape Letters* [New

York: Macmillan Publishing Co., 1961], 45-46).

Satan would love to smother our wills that he might dominate our souls. A passage from the book of Moses is arresting. Here the Lord warns Cain that "except thou shalt hearken unto my commandments, I will deliver thee up, and it shall be unto thee according to his [Satan's] desire." What did Satan want with Cain? God explained, "Satan desireth to have thee" (Moses 5:23). Satan wanted Cain for chattel. Cain was not to be his own man, but Satan's minion and sycophant. That is Satan's aim for all. Those who will follow his will, he leads "by the neck with a flaxen cord, until he bindeth them with his strong cords forever" (2 Ne. 26:22).

According to the Doctrine and Covenants, Satan flatters men and women, "and leadeth them along until he draggeth their souls down to hell; and thus he causeth them to catch themselves in their own snare. And thus he goeth up and down, to and fro in the earth, seeking to destroy the souls of men" (D&C 10:26–27). Satan wanted to destroy Cain's soul. He succeeded by catching Cain in the snare of his own greed and pride. Cain's soul became as black if not blacker than Satan's for, as God said, "from this time forth thou shalt be the father of his lies" (Moses 5:24). Cain quickly learned that misery was his lot for "Cain was shut out from the presence of God" (Moses 5:41). All who follow the same path will end up in the same place for "by the spiritual law they perish from that which is good, and become miserable forever" (2 Ne. 2:5).

It is true that God said Cain would rule over Satan (Moses 5:23). There is reason, for, as the Prophet Joseph Smith taught, "They who have tabernacles, have power over those who have not" (*Teachings*, 190). But we must put this in context. Joseph Smith also said that "all beings who have bodies have power over those who have not. The devil has no power over us only as we permit him. The moment we revolt at anything which comes from God, the devil takes power" (*Teachings*, 181). That begins now and continues into the eternal hereafter. Satan, at least to a point, even had power over Cain to make him truly miserable, but in the end, it may be Cain who is making Satan more than miserable. Of Cain's end Joseph Fielding Smith wrote,

> [T]he information given is definite that he became Perdition, and that Lucifer who is Satan, became subject to him. It appears that the reason Satan desired to have him was due to the fact that Cain had obtained a body of flesh and bones and therefore had superior power, and Satan was willing to accept and be obedient to him because of that condition. The natural conclusion is, therefore, that a devil with a body of flesh and bones has some power greater than one who was denied the physical body. (*Joseph Fielding Smith, Answers to Gospel Questions* [Salt Lake City: Deseret Book, 1958], 2:171–72).

31. Ezra Taft Benson, *Ensign*, "Mighty Change of Heart," October 1989, 2.
32. Neal A. Maxwell, *Not My Will, But Thine* (Salt Lake City: Bookcraft, 1988), 8.
33. Smith, *Teachings*, 51.

Notes to Chapter Two

1. Harold B. Lee, *Stand Ye In Holy Places* (Salt Lake City: Deseret Book, 1976), 343. The Vulgate, the Latin version of the Bible, translates the Greek (*makarios*) with *beatudo*, from which we get the term "beatitude." The King James Version of Luke 6:20–22 and Matthew 5:3–11 correctly translates the Greek *makários* with the English "blessed." Other translations, like the New International Version and Revised Standard Version use the more generic and less precise "happy."
2. The Greek word recorded by the gospel writers is the adjectival form of the verb *makarízo,* i.e. *makários.* Other words also carry the idea of blessedness, but in a secondary sense. For example: *eirēnē* ("peace"), describes the blessed state of the righteous after

earth-life; *eulogéo* ("praise" or "honor"), denotes, when pertaining to God, the favor which brings blessings and happiness to the individual; *záo* ("to live"), carries the idea of quality life, the state of active well-being and blessedness in God's eternal kingdom); *agathós* ("good"), an adjective that describes the condition of being useful, happy, pleasant, and excellent; *hypsóō* ("to lift up" or "exalt"), but in a metaphorical sense, a state of dignity, honor, or happiness). *Makários*, however, more specifically denotes the state of well-being, confidence, and assurance of one who has found favor with God. Blessedness, then, expresses the idea of a close and favored relationship between the blessed one and Deity. The transliteration of Greek forms into English follows the style found in Colin Brown, ed., *The New International Dictionary of the New Testament Theology* (Grand Rapids: Zondervan, 1975), 47. The sources for all Greek translations in this book, unless noted otherwise are: William F. Arndt and F. Wilbur Gingrich, ed. and trans., *A Greek-English Lexicon of the New Testament and other Early Christian Literature*, by Walter Bauer (Chicago: University of Chicago Press, 1979); and James H. Moulton and George Milligan, *The Vocabulary of the Greek Testament* (Grand Rapids: Eerdmans, 1985). The Greek text used is Kurt Aland, et. al., ed. of *The Greek New Testament*, 28th ed. rev. (Stuttgart, Germany: Biblia-Druck, 1994).

3. The LDS edition of the scriptures suggests the interpretation, "poor in pride, humble in spirit." Though the Greek word (*ptōchós*) used in the gospel of Matthew does not carry this meaning, the suggested reading does give insight. One of the greatest hindrances to following the Savior is pride: that Antichrist state of mind which stubbornly pits the prideful person's learning and insight against the wisdom and law of God. The proud man will learn from no one, including God, but often insists on writing his own law with the intent of forcing others to conform. In this light, the Savior points out the importance of humility—the willingness to be taught—as the beginning point of one's climb to beatitude.

4. The New Testament translates three words with the English

"mourn": *thrēnéo* (as in Matt. 11:17), meaning to bewail or lament because of the passing of another; *kóptō* (as in Matt. 24:30), meaning to beat upon the breast due to grief caused by loss or frustration; and *penthéo*, the word used in Matthew 5:4, meaning to have deep sorrow and regret.

5. Matthew used the Greek word *parákaleo*. The breadth of the word can be better understood from the context of the noun *paráklētos*. The paraklete, as the word is rendered in English, is one who pleads another's case before a judge in a court of law. In a broader sense, the word designates anyone who acts as a helper, advocate, or assistant. It is in this sense that the idea of a comforter comes to play. As one calls for help (*paráklēsis* denoting a summons, entreaty, or call for assistance), the paraklete responds and thereby brings consolation, assistance, and comfort.

6. Bruce R. McConkie, *The Mortal Messiah* (Salt Lake City: Deseret Book, 1982), 2:122.

7. The Greek word Matthew used is *praús*, which denotes a mildness of spirit and disposition grounded on one's confidence in the Lord. The meek rely on God, rather than their own strength, to overcome adversity and to direct their affairs.

8. Matthew uses the word *eleáō*, which carries the idea of kindness, compassion, and goodwill toward others, especially the less fortunate. However, the word suggests more than just kind feelings—it stresses that force which causes one to assist. It specifically applies to the Savior in His capacity of judge, when He will act mercifully toward those who have loved and served Him. Because of his mercy (*eleáō*), He will apply his grace and His Saints will stand justified before God. For insight into the relationship between mercy and righteousness, see endnote 11. It is important not to overlook mercy's forensic association. Other Greek words, translated by the English word merciful (*hílaskomai* and *oíktirmōn*), suggest the idea of compassion, pity, and goodwill, but differ from *eleáō* in two ways: they do not add the force of action, nor do they suggest that the object of the mercy is actually unworthy of it.

9. The Greek word, *xáris*, denotes kindness, graciousness, or a boon bestowed on the part of the giver. In particular, it expresses the

deep favor which one person holds for another. On the part of the receiver, it represents gratitude, thankfulness, and a sense of the favor received. The theological use has changed its meaning, but only slightly. In such a context, *xáris* has come to denote the special favorable predisposition that a god or gods feels for a person or people. Based on grace, the individual finds himself assisted by the gods in all his doings. The early Christians understood it to mean one of three things: the positive predisposition which the Father has for His children, the atoning act of the Lord, and power or assistance from the Lord, usually derived from the Holy Spirit.

10. Such a concept sheds light on certain aspects of the Savior's teachings. "The Father hath not left me alone," He pointed out, "for I do always those things that please him" (John 8:29). Here He acknowledges the contingent relationship which exists between Him and His Father. He was totally dependent upon the Father for power and knowledge. By doing God's will the Savior enjoyed communion with the Father, through which God gave grace to His Son. The Savior's profound abilities to teach and act anchored on this association. He insisted that "the Son can do nothing of himself," but "the Father that dwelleth in me, he doeth the works" (John 5:19; 14:10). Thus, the grace of God was, of necessity, upon the Son. But note that it was truly grace, for the Atonement did not affect the Father's salvation. Otherwise, any assistance God rendered could not be considered an act of grace, but of necessity.

11. The Greek adjective used in Matthew is *katharós*. The idea of lack of defilement is shared with two other Greek words (*heilikrinēs* and *hagnós*), all of which are translated by the English word "pure." *Heilikrinēs* carries the idea of being found unsullied when placed under examination. In a secondary sense, it connotes sincerity in sentiment and disposition. *Hagnós* denotes the idea of being separate or set apart from the world and dedicated to God's purpose. Its secondary meaning suggests virtue and chastity. The adjective *katharós*, on the other hand, carries the idea of that which has been purified by fire, pruned, or otherwise made fit or enhanced via a process. In a Levitical sense, it denotes that which

would not cause defilement. Of all the Greek words, this one has the broadest meaning, suggesting what is totally free from any guilt or sin. Out of this grows the accompanying ideas of blamelessness, innocence, genuineness, and that which is unstained by guilt.

12. Smith, *Teachings*, 150.

13. Ibid., 151.

14. The D&C uses the word "sanctify." The word is derived from the Latin *sanctus*, designating that which is sacred. The word has come to denote that which is set apart and that which is pure. See *Webster's New Collegiate Dictionary* (1973), s.v. sanctify.

15. Smith, *Teachings*, 151.

16. The force of my statement comes out of the nuance of the Greek text of Matthew 7:12.

17. The Book of Mormon stresses the same idea. There the Savior, after warning against anger, lust, divorce, false swearing, and so on, commanded His disciples that "ye suffer none of these things to enter into your heart; For it is better that ye should deny yourselves of these things, wherein ye will take up your cross, than that ye should be cast into hell" (3 Ne. 12:29–30). In this context, the cross is not something built by the world, but provided by the fall. It is by fighting against the natural man from day to day that one undergoes the slow crucifixion God designed as the cocoon in which the natural man is metamorphosed into a child of God.

Notes to Chapter Three

1. D&C 88:6 testifies that the Lord "ascended up on high, as also he descended below all things, in that he comprehended all things, that he might be in all and through all things, the light of truth." The Atonement allowed Him not only to obtain the heights but to suffer the depths of existence. Indeed, He was "cast into hell; into the fire that never shall be quenched, where their worm dieth not, and the fire is not quenched" (JST, Mark 9:41), and where the "torment is as a lake of fire and brimstone, whose flame ascen-

deth up forever and ever and has no end" (2 Ne. 9:16). The Atonement's power took the Lord into the full depths of hell and heaped upon Him all the embarrassment, shame, remorse, guilt of conscience, and suffering of all sinners, "which suffering caused myself, even God, the greatest of all, to tremble because of pain, and to bleed at every pore, and to suffer both body and spirit— and would that I might not drink the bitter cup, and shrink" (D&C 19:18). For Him, the fires of hell waxed their hottest.

2. The Greek word *doûlos* identifies one in a servile condition, especially a slave or bondsman. Another word translated as "servant," *diàkonos* (as in Matthew 22:13: 23:11; John 12:26), means a waiter or minister—one who is paid for services rendered.

3. The temples of Babylon and Egypt held lands and engaged in manufacturing. Therefore, they employed many slaves out of necessity. For a general study, see Marvin A. Dandameav, *Slavery in Babylonia from Nabopoloassar to Alexander the Great (626-331)*, trans. Victoria A. Powell (DeKalb, Illinois: Northern Illinois University, 1984), and Isaac Mendelsohn, *Slavery in the Ancient Near East* (New York: Liberal Arts Press, 1949). For the early Christian period, see M. I. Finley, *The Ancient Economy* (Berkeley: University of California Press, 1973), especially pp. 62–94.

4. Paul does this in Romans 1:1 and Titus 1:1; Peter in 2 Peter 1:1 and John in Revelation 1:1. See also William Rollins, "Greco-Roman Slave Terminology and Pauline Metaphors for Salvation," *Society of Biblical Literature Seminar Papers*, ed. K. H. Richards (Atlanta: Society of Biblical Literature, 1987), 100-109.

5. The first epistle of John has two stated objectives. One is to show the people how to achieve joy, the other "fellowship." The Greek term that John used, *koinonía*, translated as "fellowship" in the KJV, carries the idea of sharing in common, or achieving equality. Therefore, when he says, "That which we have seen and heard declare we unto you, that ye also may have fellowship with us: and truly our fellowship is with the Father, and with his Son Jesus Christ" (1 Jn 1:3), he shows that some kind of condition of equality can be set up between saint, apostle, Son, and Father.

6. The Greek word *phílos* carries the idea of a confidante, friend, and

close companion.

7. See full discussion and references below.

8. *A New Witness for the Articles of Faith* (Salt Lake City: Deseret Book, 1985), 131.

9. Bruce R. McConkie, "Households of Faith," *Speeches of the Year* (Provo, Utah: Brigham Young University Press, 1970), 5.

10. Ibid., 5-6.

11. Luke does say that "there appeared an angel unto him from heaven, strengthening him." However, this angelic assistance brought no relief, for He, "being in an agony . . . prayed more earnestly: and his sweat was as it were great drops of blood falling down to the ground" (Luke 22:43–44). Only assistance from the omnipotence of the Father would do, and that was not forth-coming.

12. Brigham Young, et. al., *Journal of Discourses* (Liverpool: Orson Pratt, 1856), 13:206.

13. The Joseph Smith Translation gives this account a different cast. According to the JST, "they came to a place which was named Gethsemane, which was a garden; and the disciples began to be sore amazed, and to be very heavy, and to complain in their hearts, wondering if this be the Messiah" (JST, Mark 14:36). Here it is the disciples which were sore amazed and troubled. Still, nothing precludes the idea that the trial did not astonish the Savior as well.

14. The Greek word (*ekthambéō*) means to be amazed in the sense of alarmed. The adjective form (*ékthambos*) translates as "utterly astonished."

15. Neal A. Maxwell, Conference Report, April 1985, 92. (Conference Reports will be cited hereafter as CR.)

16. Some see the statement that "it is by grace we are saved, after all we can do" (2 Ne. 25:23) as meaning that grace kicks in only after we have done our part. Stephen E. Robinson argues that the word "after" should be taken as a preposition of separation rather than one of time. "It denotes logical separateness," he observes, "rather than temporal sequence. We are saved by grace 'apart from all we

can do,' or 'all we can do notwithstanding,' or even 'regardless of all we can do.' Another acceptable paraphrase of the sense of the verse might read, 'We are still saved by grace, after all is said and done.'" See *Believing Christ* (Salt Lake City: Deseret Book, 1992), 91–92.

Notes to Chapter Four

1. The Greek is *hilasmos*. It is of note that John does not say how the Lord accomplished the expiation, but neither in 1 John 2:2 nor 4:10 does he mention His death. It is the risen Lord who is the expiator (2:1 and 4:10). So the expiation comes not out of the Savior's death alone, but out of the totality of His ministry, including His resurrection. That means His teachings, ministry, death, resurrection, and power make up His *hilasmos*.

2. It is from the Septuagint, the Old Testament translated into Greek some time before Christ, that we see what the word *hilasmos* meant to the early Christians. The word translates from the Hebrew *chafar*. As used in Genesis 20:16; 32:21; and Job 9:24, it carried the idea of covering over, or, in a religious sense, making expiation. Through the act, injury was made good and the injured party reconciled to the guilty. The word denoted that act by which the hurt was covered over, allowing the guilty party to be released from all further obligation. But, when it came to God, human guilt demanded spiritual death—separation from God forever. In this case, it was God, the Savior, who both made and granted the expiation without which sinful man must die. For a full discussion, see Gerhard Kittel, ed., Geoffry W. Bromiley, trans., *Theological Dictionary of the New Testament* (Grand Rapids: Eerdmans, 1964), s.v. *hileōs*. (This work will be cited hereafter as *TDNT*.)

3. The Greek word *dynamis* denotes ability and power, and is usually translated with the English "power." See Matt. 6:13; Mark 9:1; 13:25; Luke 1:17; 9:1. *Exousia* means privilege or authority, and is usually translated as "authority." See Matt. 9:6; 28:18; Mark 2:10; 6:7; Luke 4:6; 10:19; 19:17.

4. We must understand that *exousia*, generally meaning "privilege" or "authority," differs from the word *dymamis*, usually translated

"power" in the KJV. The latter denotes intrinsic ability while the former emphasizes the ability to perform an action which removes all hindrances in accomplishing what must be done. It also defines the rights granted by a higher norm or court by which one is given authority, permission, or freedom. *Dynamis* connotes external power or force over which one has little or no control, while *exousia* connotes the delegated inner power which the individual controls. When associated with God, *exousia* denotes the invincible power of God which gives Him Lordship over this fallen world in which nothing takes place apart from His authority. In Revelation, the *exousia* of God controls and sets the limits of destruction. For example, see Rev. 9:3, 10, 19. The use of the word here emphasizes that even the locusts' or scorpions' power to hurt is lent them by God. God also extends his *exousia* to the Son and from Him to the Lord's apostles and disciples. It is by God's *exousia* abiding in them that the Apostles have *dynamis* in and over the world. For a more full discussion, see Kittel, *TDNT*, s.v. *exestin*.

5. The word "authority," in the King James text, is a translation of *exousia* in every case except 1 Timothy 2:2 and Titus 2:15.

6. Kittel, *TDNT*, s.v. *exestin*.

7. The Greek word *tēreō* means "to watch over," "protect," and "to guard." It expresses the idea of taking care of something cherished or of worth.

8. Both Peter and Paul were well aware that revelation and spiritual knowledge did not assure one against losing the reward. Both warned that, for those who sinned after tasting of the sweet things of God, there would be no sacrifice which would expiate their sins. See 2 Peter 2:20-22; Heb. 6:4-6; 10:26-27; D&C 76:31-38.

9. That all the synoptic writers relate this miracle (Matthew 9:20-22; Luke 8:43–48) underscores its importance.

10. See Lev. 15:19–27. The Mishnah, in the section dealing with these verses, refers to a woman suffering from a discharge of blood as *zabah*. Because menses and associated disorders were causes for ceremonial uncleanliness, an entire tractate, *Zabim*, was devoted to it.

11. The source of the idea comes out of rabbinical extrapolations of

Leviticus 5:2–4. See Mishnah, *Shebuoth*, 1.1–4.

12. Eusebius, *Ecclesiastical History* (Grand Rapids, Michigan: Baker Book House, 1955), 7.18. Apocryphal sources embellished the account, giving her the name Bernice (in Greek) or Veronica (in Latin). See *Acts of Pilate*, 7, and William L. Lane, *The Gospel of Mark* of *The New International Commentary on the New Testament* (Grand Rapids: Eerdmans, 1974), 194.

13. According to James E. Talmage,

> The faith of those who believed that if they could but touch the border of the Lord's garment they would be healed, is in line with that of the woman who was healed of her long-standing malady by so touching His robe (see Matt. 9:21; Mark 5:27, 28; Luke 8:44). The Jews regarded the border or hem of their outer robes as of particular importance, because of the requirement made of Israel in earlier days (Num. 15:38, 39) that the border be fringed and supplied with a band of blue, as a reminder to them of their obligations as the covenant people. The desire to touch the hem of Christ's robe may have been associated with this thought of sanctity attaching to the hem or border (*Jesus the Christ* [Salt Lake City: Deseret Book, 1947], 346–47).

14. The Greek *aretē* is the word usually translated as "virtue," but in this case it is *dynamis*.

15. In all three accounts, the Lord addresses the woman by this insightful title. It is of note that nowhere else does the Lord address a woman as a father to a child.

16. W. Robertson Nicoll, ed., *The Expositor's Greek Testament* (Grand Rapids: Eerdmans, n.d.), 1:376.

17. Smith, *Teachings*, 298.

18. The word translated "suffer" in this passage (Greek *páthos*) denotes the vicissitudes through which we in mortality go. Thus, it can be rendered "experience," but it generally suggests misfortune or calamity.

Notes to Chapter Five

1. Günther Bornkamm, *Paulus*, (Stuttgart: W. Kohlhammer Verlag, 1969), 222, correctly notes that "dieses Wort wie kaum ein anderes in den christlichen Sprachschatz eingegangen ist und— unendlich oft gebraucht und mißbraucht—weithin seinen Inhalt und seine Kraft verloren hat." (To translate: "This word, almost more than any other, has entered into the vocabulary of Christians and—quite often used and misused—has largely lost its meaning and force.")

2. Lean Morris, *Testaments of Love* (Michigan: Eerdmans, 1981), 3.

3. Ancient Greek was rich in words for love and can, therefore, provide the modern inquirer with a way to understand with precision certain nuances the word held anciently that might otherwise pass beyond him, such as *eunoia, epithymia, philia, thelō, agapē, erōs, storgē*. Three words deserve a note because each expresses a dimension of love and is used by the New Testament writers. However, since none of them are translated as "love" in the KJV, and also because they contribute only a small degree to our understanding of love, I do not feel they need to be developed in the body of the text. The first word is the Greek *epithymia*. It denoted an intense desire and was often associated with strong passion. The Greeks used it to describe both positive and negative feelings. The New Testament follows suit. On the negative side, John warns against the "lust of the flesh" (1 Jn. 2:16), and Paul cautions the Saint not to give in to "evil passions" (Col. 3:5). On the positive side, the Savior used it to explain the deep yearning the Old Testament prophets had to see the day of His earthly ministry (see Matt. 13:17), and how much He ached to celebrate the Passover with his friends (see Luke 22:15). See Morris, *Testaments*, 119–20, and *TNDT*, s.v. *epithymia* and *epithymētēs*. The second word is the Greek *thelō*. The word expresses "will," "desire," or "devotion." Like *epithymia*, it had both a negative and positive aspect. The negative side expressed the idea of desire, lust, or pleasure in an erotic sense. The positive side denoted "to like" or "take pleasure in," and "to will" another's good. For example, in 1 Timothy 4:8 it expresses God's passionate desire to save all, and in Matthew 15:32 it conveys the Savior's wish to assist those

who follow Him. See *TDNT*, s.v. *thelō*, and also Ceslaus Spicq, *Agapē in the New Testament* (St. Louis: B. Harder Book, 1963), 1:39. The last word, *eunoia*, meant "to be well-disposed" toward, to be on "friendly" terms with and carried the idea of close attachment. It had no negative aspect. Its meaning is expressed in the Savior's demand that His disciple have goodwill toward an adversary (Matt. 5:25), and in Paul's admonition that the household servants show kindness toward their masters (Eph. 6:7). See *TDNT*, s.v. *eunoia* covered under *nous*, and Spicq, *Agapē*, 1:39, where he treats the related term *eudokeo*.

4. *The Greek word is storgē. Philia*, more directly than *storgē*, denoted that love associated with friendship, especially that between persons of the same gender, but without sexual connotation. It does not appear in the Bible except in the compound *philadelphia*, brotherly love. For a good discussion on the association and importance of these words in understanding love see C. S. Lewis, *The Four Loves* (New York: Harcourt Brace Jovanovich, 1960), 53–83.

5. Paul used the Greek word, *astorgos*.

6. Compare this with W. Barclay's insistence that "the Greek word *storgē* is the word which is used especially of *family love*, the love of child for parent and parent for child. If there is no human affection, then the family cannot exist" (*The Letters to Timothy, Titus, and Philemon* [Philadelphia: Westminister Press, 1960], 216).

7. The Greek word translated "love" here is *agapē*, the favorite form of the word in the New Testament. However, as is shown below, it has a strong tie to *storgē*.

8. In this regard, see D&C 45:26–27.

9. Lewis, *The Four Loves*, 67.

10. I have here extended the meaning more than first century Christian documents actually allow. Nonetheless, the spirit of what I have stressed is correct and helps us to see why *storgē* must be promoted and practiced.

11. The word is not found in the New Testament. We only see it in its negative aspect, *astorgos*, meaning "unloving," in Romans 1:31;

Titus 3:3.

12. The word the scriptures use is *agapētos*, see Matt. 3:17; 17:5; Mark 9:7 for examples. By using the term they did, the writers of the Gospels expressed an important element in the relationship between the Father and the Son. The word suggests that God does not reach down to His Son as a mortal father to his little one with a rush of warm, protecting, and benevolent feeling. The Father's words suggest a relationship of near equality showing the Father's intent to honor the Son. Of note also is that the first time the word "love" appears in the New Testament, at the Savior's baptism, it marks the proclamation of the divinity of the Savior and of His standing as God's beloved. "On the banks of the Jordan he named Jesus his son, and his *agapētos*, his beloved. Clearly, *agapē* exists in God; it is the force uniting the two divine Persons unchangeably, from all eternity" (Spicq, *Agape*, 1:39, 49)

13. Morris, *Testaments*, 116–17.

14. The Greek word is *erōs*.

15. James Moffatt thinks this makes the word unattractive to New Testament writers: "In spite of its devotional possibilities, the term had been compromised by its lower associations of sensuous desire and lust" (*Love in the New Testament*, [London: Hodder and Stoughton, 1929], 38).

16. Plato emphasizes this in the speech of Pausanius. He stresses the point that there are two loves, the popular and the heavenly (*Symposium*, 180D). It is the heavenly that is pure *ers*. Compare also the two horses in the figure employed by Socrates (*Phaedrus*, 253C-254A). Plato speaks of love as "desire" and "a kind of madness" (*Phaedrus*, 273D, 265A), and also as a tyrant (*Republic*, 573B). Clearly he sees many possibilities in *erōs*.

17. An example might be the "courtly love" of the Middle Ages, "whose characteristics may be enumerated as Humility, Courtesy, Adultery, and the Religion of Love" (C. S. Lewis, *The Allegory of Love* [London: Oxford University Press, 1936], 2). There is a good deal that is attractive in this love, but also much that is unattractive—for example, the abjectness of the typical lover and the insistence on adultery.

18. Morris, *Testaments*, 120–21.

19. Ibid.

20. Ibid., 122.

21. The Greek word is *philia*.

22. Denis de Rougemont, in his work *Love Declared,* New York: Pantheon Books, 1963, 6, especially note 3, investigates the breadth of the word as used by ancient philosophers. Though the basic meaning is that of affection between two persons, the philosophers saw four types: that which best described true friendship; that associated with parent and child relationships (*physikè*), and uniting those with common blood; that between host and guest (*xenikè*), expressed in hospitality; and an amorous love (*erotikè*), expressed between persons of the same or opposite gender. See also Morris, *Testaments*, 117–18.

23. Cicero, *De Amicitia*; Aristotle, *Magna Moralia*, see especially *Ethica Nicomachea* 1166.31, that notes that a friend is but another self.

24. Lewis, *The Four Loves*, 88, 103.

25. Ibid., 104.

26. Ibid., 115.

27. Morris, *Testaments*, 118-19.

28. The Greek word is *phileō*.

29. John uses the word *philous*, confidante, close friend.

30. Actually, the gospel writers show little distinction between the meaning of *phileō* and *agapē*. Both express the ideal love commended by the Savior. For a comprehensive study, see Roy F. Butler, *The Meaning of* Agapao *and* Phileo *in the Greek New Testament* (Lawrence, Kansas: Coronado Press, 1977).

In this regard, a note on one scriptural passage seems in order because a number of Biblical commentators have made more of it than they should. After His Resurrection, the Lord appeared to His disciples on the shores of the Sea of Galilee. There, according to John,

Jesus saith to Simon Peter, Simon, son of Jonas, lovest [agapaō] thou me more than these? He saith unto him, Yea,

Lord; thou knowest that I love [phileō] thee. He saith unto him, Feed my lambs. He saith to him again the second time, Simon, son of Jonas, lovest [agapaō] thou me? He saith unto him, Yea, Lord; thou knowest that I love [phileō] thee. He saith unto him, Feed my sheep. He saith unto him the third time, Simon, son of Jonas, lovest [phileō] thou me? Peter was grieved because he said unto him the third time, Lovest [phileō] thou me? And he said unto him, Lord, thou knowest all things; thou knowest that I love [phileō] thee. Jesus saith unto him, Feed my sheep (John 21:15–17).

Some see the Savior asking for a pure Christian love *(agapaō)* and Peter confessing to a lesser love *(phileō)*. The Lord finally condescends to accept this lesser love. An excellent example of this kind of misunderstanding can be found in the Greek lexicon of *LDS Collectors Library for Windows* (Provo, Utah: Infobases, 1997), s. v. "love", in John 21:15 where an argument is made that *agapao* is somehow a higher and holier form of love than *phileō*. Such is not the case. John was simply using synonyms to express the interaction between the Savior and Peter.

31. The Greek word is *agapē*.

32. *TDNT*, I, 37. The verb form of the word, *agapaō*, however, was very common. It is the use of the noun that was unusual.

33. It occurs in Aristeas 229; Phil, *Quod Deus Imm.* 69; Testament of Reuben 6.9; Gad 4.2; 6; 7; 5.2; Asher 2.4; Joseph 17.3; Benjamin 3.5; 8.1, 2; Sib. Or. 2.65, 6.25; Ps. Sol. 18.4.

34. Of course the linguistics do not prove the point. The Christian idea of love is best defined in books where the word *agapē* is not found. The meaning is derived from the way the Christians defined love, not from the word they chose to express it. In fact the opposite is true, for their definition would have prevailed with whatever word they used. However, their choice of a more obscure word, unladen with the trappings of heavy use, better allowed them to put their own twist on it. On this, see Morris, *Testaments*, 125–27.

35. In general, secular Greek defined the verb *agapaō* as much more colorless than either *erōs* or *phileō,* and some scholars believe that in that context it carries the feeling of "prefer." For a full discussion, see *TDNT*, I, 37.

36. Morris, *Testaments*, 128.

37. Ibid. I have heard some make quite a bit out of the differences between charity (Greek *agapē*) and friendship (Greek *phileō*), but the two words were used interchangeably.

38. For a discussion, see Anders Nygren, *Agape and Eros* (Philadelphia: Westminister Press, 1953), 68.

39. The word he used, *ālthon*, is the aorist or simple past form of *érxomai.*

40. Morris, *Testaments,* 148–49.

41. Because of the way the KJV reads, many visualize these men ripping a huge hole in the roof off the house. This, however, is not the case. Roofs on these houses were very sturdy and the labor to break through one would have taken both time and effort, not to mention bringing down the ire of the homeowner. The Greek word used by Luke, *keramos*, refers to earthenware and, therefore, to roof tiling. However, by extension, the word referred to any covering and, more especially, to that of an awning. It seems the men broke out part of the awning, often made of poles and palm leaves, covering the courtyard. Such an act would have taken little time or effort and left a hole easily repaired.

42. Charles Cutler Torrey, *The Four Gospels* (New York: Harper and Brothers, 1933), 291. The context of the commandment to "be perfect" is that of love. (See Matt. 5:44–48.) The Book of Mormon underscores the idea. After the Lord commands his disciples to "love your enemies, bless them that curse you, do good to them that hate you," he adds that in him "old things are done away, and all things have become new." That includes the command to love. He has added a dimension that the word did not carry under the old law. With the added dimension, the commandment has become new and complete. (See 3 Ne. 12:44-48.)

43. The Greek word is *dēnarius.*

44. The Jerusalem Talmud, *Berak.* 2.5c, as found in A. H. M'Neile,

The Gospel According to St. Matthew (London: Macmillan, 1915), 285. The parable is also found in Ecclesiastes Rabbah and in Song of Songs Rabbah, suggesting that the rabbis felt its message had real value.

45. Ibid.

46. Morris, *Testaments*, 156.

47. Ibid., 155-56.

48. Ibid., 163.

49. Unfortunately, I cannot remember where I heard or read it, but the parable is not mine.

Notes to Chapter Six

1. Smith, *Teachings*, 301.

2. Peter had known for over thirty years that he would die a martyr. On the banks of the Sea of Galilee, shortly after the Lord's resurrection, the Savior had prophesied, "When thou wast young, thou girdedst thyself, and walkedst whither thou wouldest: but when thou shalt be old, thou shalt stretch forth thy hands, and another shall gird thee, and carry thee whither thou wouldest not." Then says John, "This spake he [Jesus], signifying by what death he [Peter] should glorify God" (John 21:18–19).

3. The phrase is *diegeírein hymás en hypomnēsei,* literally, "to arouse you by way of reminder."

4. The word *kaléō,* from ancient secular Greek, means "to call to, summon, or invite." In the New Testament usage, it is the latter that is almost always intended. The writers of the New Testament books use the word uniformly to express the idea that God calls or invites individuals through the Savior to do His work. The call is always to faith and obedience, but with the objective in mind to achieve godly glory and eternal life. Therefore, the word, as used in the New Testament, takes on a technical nature associated with the process of exaltation. See *TDNT,* s.v. *kaléō;* Bruce R. McConkie, *Doctrinal New Testament Commentary* (Salt Lake City: Bookcraft, 1973), 3:326–29, hereafter noted as *DNTC.*

5. McConkie, *DNTC,* 3:329.

6. Ibid., 326–27.

7. The Greek verb *eklegō* means "to pick out," "choose," or "select." In a theological sense, it denotes God's selection of a certain person or people to carry out His will here on earth. Thus, the Messiah is the elect of God being chosen to hold the most exalted position. Peter uses the adjectival form *eklektos* to indicate a person chosen by merit or worth.

8. Elder McConkie notes that the term applies more expressly to that select group of Saints who strive with all their hearts to keep their covenants, live the gospel law, and magnify their callings (*DNTC*, 3:329).

9. Ibid., 3:329–30.

10. The word Paul used, *proorízō*, means "to determine before hand," "preordain," or, in Latter-day Saint terminology, "to foreordain." The idea conveyed by the word is much stronger than most Latter-day Saints allow. Because of our desire to quash any nuance of predeterminism, a concept that denies agency, we are often guilty of not giving sufficient credit to the power of foreordination. Though it cannot overrule agency, it does mean that God has set everything in place for the agent's success. Additionally, this premortal ordination goes a long way toward moving a person in a direction prechosen by God. The scriptures provide us with two examples. The first is Alma the Younger. While he was yet trying to destroy the Church, an angel appeared and brought him to the right path. In this we see one father's prayer and another Father's foreordination at play (see Mosiah 27:14). The second is Paul. He could never forget that at the very moment of his call, he was persecuting his Lord by trying to destroy His Church. His only explanation for his redemption was that "it pleased God, who separated me from my mother's womb, and called me by his grace" (Gal. 1:15). In other words, before he was born, God separated him out for his special ministry. That separation, coupled with the power of grace, overlooked his current course of action and allowed him, for the moment, to be brought into divine favor. Through that, the Lord extended the call to service. Paul did not have to accept the call, but foreordination determined that the call would be extended and, perhaps, even

dictated the startling way in which it would come.

11. Joseph Smith stated that "the things that are written are only hints of things which existed in the prophet's mind, which are not written concerning eternal glory" (*Teachings*, 304).

12. The KJV also translates *oida*, "to see, perceive, or know"; *sunesis*, "to understand"; and *epistēmōn,* "to understand or be intelligent," with the English "knowledge."

13. The word for "knowledge" that denotes acquaintanceship with some subject in general is *gnōsis*. Peter uses the form *epignōsis*, which denotes full or complete knowledge. Such knowledge extends beyond study to that learned by experience.

14. Smith, *Teachings*, 297. See also Andrew Ehat and Lyndon Cook, ed., *The Words of Joseph Smith* (Provo, Utah: Religious Studies Center, Brigham Young University, 1980), 200.

15. For a discussion of the power of grace in assisting to overcome the world and gaining association in the divine family, see Hyrum L. Andrus, *Principles of Perfection* (Salt Lake City: Bookcraft, 1970), 202–03, and Robinson, *Believing Christ*, 61-69. The idea behind the Greek *ierēnē*, peace, as used in the Christian context, extended the meaning beyond the idea of harmony, tranquility, or quiet. Influenced by the Hebrew *šhalōm*, the word carried the idea of peace with God and His chosen people through covenantal association with Him. For an excellent discussion of peace in the context of the gospel, see Marion G. Romney, CR, October, 1949, 39–41.

16. For a full discussion, see Richard D. Draper, "Light, Truth, and Grace: Three Interrelated Salvation Themes in D&C 93," H. Dean Garrett, ed., *Doctrines for Exaltation* (Salt Lake City: Deseret Book, 1989), 29–41.

17. Note D&C 93:24. The LDS hymn, "Oh Say, What Is Truth?" defines truth as "the sum of existence." See *Hymns of The Church of Jesus Christ of Latter-day Saints* (Salt Lake City: Deseret Book, 1985), 272.

18. Draper, "Light, Truth, and Grace," 24–31.

19. Brent L. and Wendy C. Top, *Beyond Death's Door: Understanding Near-Death Experiences in Light of the Restored Gospel* (Salt Lake

City: Bookcraft, 1993), 90. For the complete study, see pages 88–90.

20. The majority of Greek texts state that we receive these things through the knowledge of him *tou kalesantos hēmas idia doksēkai aretē.* The words "his own," given in my translation of the text, though appearing in many ancient Greek texts, were not translated into the King James Bible. Only a few ancient texts replace *idia* ("his own") with *dia* ("to" or "through").

21. That is, *epignōsis.*

22. That is, *epignōsis.*

23. The Greek text underscores the stress Peter put on the idea. His use of the phrase *kai auto touto* ("for this very reason") underscores his admonition. I would translate it as, "Because you can do this, then make every effort to supplement your faith with moral excellence."

24. Romney, CR, October, 1949, 43.

25. The word used here is *gnōsis.*

26. That is, *gnōsis.*

27. The word is *egkrateia,* which is composed of *en* (in) and *krateō* (powerful, strong, mighty).

28. The need for patience to become godlike will not end at resurrection. The attributes and the powers of the Father are so vast that further development will be necessary even for those who are celestial. Consider Joseph Smith's statement that,

> *when you climb up a ladder, you must begin at the bottom, and ascend step by step, until you arrive at the top; and so it is with the principles of the Gospel—you must begin with the first, and go on until you learn all the principles of exaltation. But it will be a great while after you have passed through the veil before you will have learned them. It is not all* to be comprehended in this world; *it will be a great work to learn our salvation and exaltation even beyond the grave* (*Teachings,* 348, italics in the original).

29. *Eusebeiais* expresses the idea of having deep reverence for one's gods.

30. The Greek word used by Paul, *anastrophē*, is regularly translated as "conversation" in the KJV, but carries the meaning of conduct, behavior, or manner of life.
31. The Christian understanding of *hagios,* "holy," corresponds with the Hebrew *qadôš*. Both words denote the separation of God and, hopefully, His children from the mundane and worldly.
32. James says much the same thing as John: "Know ye not that the friendship of the world is enmity with God? whosoever therefore will be a friend of the world is the enemy of God" (James 4:4). Hugh Nibley makes a good point on this, saying,

> I live in the real world, don't I? Yes, and I have been commanded to "come out of her, . . . that ye be not partakers of her sins" (Revelation 18:4). It is not given "unto you that ye shall live after the manner of the world" (D&C 95:13). Well, then, you must be "in the world but not of the world." That happens to be a convenient para-scripture (we have quite a few of them today), invented by a third-century Sophist (Diognetos), to the great satisfaction of the church members, who were rapidly becoming very worldly (*Collected Works of Hugh Nibley*, vol. 9, *Approaching Zion* [Salt Lake City, Deseret Book, 1989], 164–65).

Most, however, who quote this "para-scripture" do not use it to contradict John. They generally mean that though we must live on the earth, we are not to take part in the materialism, greed, sensuality, and other seductive forces which operate therein. That is precisely John's point.

33. The word is *agapē*.
34. That is, *epígnōsis*.
35. The King James text is a bit misleading when it says, "We have also a more sure word of prophecy." The Greek is *kai exomen bebaioteron ton prophētikon logon*, "And we have the prophetic word made certain." *Bebaioteron*, the comparative adjective of *bebaios*, carries the idea of "firm, certain, permanent."

36. John Taylor, *Journal of Discourses* (Liverpool: John Henry Smith, 1884), 24:85.

37. Brigham Young, *Journal of Discourses* (Liverpool: Albert Carrington, 1869), 12:65.

38. See, for example, Romney, *CR*, October 1949, 39–45, and April 1977, 59–63; L. G. Otten and C. M. Caldwell, *Sacred Truths of the Doctrine & Covenants* (Springville, Utah: LEMB, Inc., 1983), 2:349–50.

39. Charles W. Nibley, *CR*, April 1927, 27.

40. Smith, *Teachings*, 298.

41. Joseph Fielding Smith, *Doctrines of Salvation* (Salt Lake City: Bookcraft, 1954), 1:45, italics in the original. McConkie, *DNTC*, 3:334, states that one of the functions of the Holy Ghost is to seal or ratify the promised blessings associated with baptism, priesthood ordination, or marriage, upon the individual or couple. Elder Smith emphasized that "if a person violates a covenant, whether it be of baptism, ordination, marriage or anything else, the Spirit withdraws the stamp of approval, and the blessings will not be received" (*Doctrines*, 1:45). In another place he explained that:

> [E]very covenant, contract, bond, obligation, oath, vow, and performance, that man receives through the covenants and blessings of the gospel, is sealed by the Holy Spirit with a promise. The promise is that the blessing will be obtained, if those who seek it are true and faithful to the end. If they are not faithful, then the Holy Spirit will withdraw the blessing, and the promise comes to an end (Ibid., 2:94–95).

42. At one time, stake presidents had the opportunity of nominating people for a special priesthood blessing. The President of the Church would then approve the nomination. This is no longer the case. Instructions to the stake presidents stated that "the individuals selected must not be informed until after the issuance of such recommends. As a general rule, such recommends are issued only in behalf of those who have had endowments in lifetime,

and have been sealed and lived together faithfully as husband and wife, and who have been valiant in the defense of truth and active in all good works" (James R. Clark, ed., *Messages of the First Presidency* [Salt Lake City: Bookcraft, 1971], 5:112). Note that the couple were not informed until after the recommend was issued. Further, the blessing was given only after valiance and good works were proved. These people had long before entered into covenants with the Lord which were sealed, along with the blessings, by the Holy Spirit of Promise. The priesthood blessing confirmed the sealing and made the promises sure, but that sealing itself took place the moment the couple first made the covenants and the sealing continued, albeit conditionally, because they faithfully fulfilled their commitments. That the sealing becomes unconditional through this blessing can be seen in the following message from the ninth general epistle dated April 13, 1853:

> Think not, O ye Elders of Israel! that your eternal heirship is won, and immutably secured, because you have attained to a portion of the Holy Priesthood, and few of its initiating ordinances, while as yet your life and the security of all your great and glorious blessings in hope and prospect, are as a vapour before the sun; as yet depending wholly on your meekness, faithfulness, and perseverance to the *end*, in *everything good*. Think not that you are legally entitled to even *one life*, while you live on this earth, unless you are sealed up to *everlasting lives*, by the will and *decree* of the *Eternal Father*, and a knowledge of the fact has been communicated to you, through the *proper source*, and not *direct*, to *you*, in *person*. And consider that the blessings you have hitherto received, through the mercies of Him who loveth you, even your Father in heaven, will all be *wrested* from you, like *David's* of old, should you err like him (Ibid., 2:117, italics in original).

This epistle shows that being sealed to everlasting life secures the blessings, but that it is confirmed to the individual through the proper priesthood channels and can still be lost if a person is unfaithful.

43. Lee, *Stand Ye in Holy Places*, 32. (See 1 Pet. 1:8–9.)

44. The word *tēréō* carries the idea of watching over something of value, thus, being constantly on guard.

45. Smith, *Teachings*, 9. (The statement comes in a report of 25 October 1831; *Far West Record: Minutes of The Church of Jesus Christ of Latter-day Saints, 1830–1844*, ed. Donald Q. Cannon and Lyndon W. Cook [Salt Lake City: Deseret Book, 1983], 23).

46. There is some question about when a person's name is written in the Lamb's book of life. Joseph Smith suggested that the act takes place after a person has shown tremendous faith in God and sacrificed much in his service (*Teachings*, 8). Brigham Young believed that the names of all the sons and daughters of Adam were written in the book, but if they did not accept the gospel and live its teachings, their names would be blotted out (*Discourses of Brigham Young* (Salt Lake City: Deseret Book, 1954), 5, 7, 387-88). Joseph Fielding Smith believed it took more than membership in the Church, but continued faithfulness and commandment keeping. (*Doctrines of Salvation*, 2:14). All seem to agree that the book is a literal record kept in heaven of a person's covenants and righteous deeds (see Ps. 69:28; Rev. 3:5; 21:27; D&C 128:6–7). All whose names appear there at the judgment receive eternal life (D&C 76:68; 132:19). It is clear that acceptance of the gospel, making and keeping covenants, and enduring in faithful service are required to keep one's name there.

47. Smith, *Teachings*, 9. The statement as recorded in the *Teachings* is vague. The source is a scribe's synopsis of the meeting at which the Prophet was speaking (see *Teachings*, 9, note 5). If the Prophet was keeping his points parallel, the context suggests that he was noting that certain things grow out of having one's name written in the Lamb's book of life: the Saint will have perfect love, false Christs will not deceive him, and he will never fall. However, he may have been saying that certain things flow out of having perfect love: one's name is written in the Lamb's book of life, false Christs will not deceive him, and he will never fall. Since the context of the talk is taking care of others and supporting them

with physical necessities, it seems that the Prophet was showing the Saints what could grow out of their love.

48. Smith, *Teachings*, 338–39.

49. Leaving the love of Christ to follow forbidden paths costs these souls their eternal lives, but it does not cost them salvation. Joseph Smith taught that:

> [A]ll sin, and all blasphemies, and every transgression, except one, that man can be guilty of, may be forgiven; and there is a salvation for all men, either in this world or the world to come, who have not committed the unpardonable sin, there being a provision either in this world or the world of spirits. Hence God hath made a provision that every spirit in the eternal world can be ferreted out and saved unless he has committed that unpardonable sin which cannot be remitted to him either in this world or the world of spirits (*Teachings,* 356).

Expanding on this idea, the Prophet said, "All are within the reach of pardoning mercy, who have not committed the unpardonable sin, which hath no forgiveness, neither in this world, nor in the world to come" (Ibid., 191–92). He clarified that "the unpardonable sin is to shed innocent blood, or be accessory thereto" (Ibid., 301), and that "a man cannot commit the unpardonable sin after the dissolution of the body, and there is a way possible for escape" (Ibid., 357).

Another sin falling into the camp of unpardonable is that of denying the Holy Ghost. Of this the Prophet said:

> All sins shall be forgiven, except the sin against the Holy Ghost; for Jesus will save all except the sons of perdition. What must a man do to commit the unpardonable sin? He must receive the Holy Ghost, have the heavens opened unto him, and know God, and then sin against Him. After a man has sinned against the Holy Ghost, there is no repentance for him. He has got to say that the sun does not

shine while he sees it; he has got to deny Jesus Christ when
the heavens have been opened unto him, and to deny the
plan of salvation with his eyes open to the truth of it; and
from that time he begins to be an enemy. This is the case
with many apostates of the Church of Jesus Christ of
Latter-day Saints (Ibid., 358).

Such a soul turns his back on love and *epignōsis*. In doing so, he hardens his heart to the point that it can never become contrite, broken, and saved.

50. The Greek term for a down payment was *arrabōn*. The *arrabōn* acted as the promise that the purchaser would make full payment on the item, but it also assured him that seller would not sell the item to another. The word must not be confused with other words also translated as "earnest" in the KJV. These are *epipothesis* describing "desire," or "longing," as in 2 Corinthians 7:7; *apokaradokia,* meaning anxious or continued expectation, as in Romans 8:19 and Philippians 1:20; *spoudē,* denoting diligent striving as in 2 Corinthians 8:16; and finally, *perissoteros,* suggesting more abundant or earnest effort, as in Hebrews 2:1.

51. Some mistakenly believe that D&C 132:19–20, 26–27 assures individuals that, if sealed by the Holy Spirit of promise, they will obtain heaven without service, sacrifice, and righteousness, that they can get away with any sin or transgression, as long as they don't commit murder. Two flaws mark this kind of thinking.

First, Joseph Smith taught that there is a limit on what the Spirit can seal:

> If men sin wilfully after they have received the knowl-
> edge of the truth, there remaineth no more sacrifice for sin,
> but a certain fearful looking for of judgment and fiery
> indignation to come, which shall devour these adversaries.
> For he who despised Moses' law died without mercy under
> two or three witnesses. Of how much more severe punish-
> ment suppose ye, shall he be thought worthy, who hath sold
> his brother, and denied the new and everlasting covenant by

which he was sanctified, calling it an unholy thing, and
doing despite to the Spirit of grace (*Teachings,* 128).

He further declared that "so long as a man will not give heed to
the commandments, he must abide without salvation. If a man
has knowledge, he can be saved; although, if he has been guilty of
great sins, he will be punished for them. But when he consents to
obey the Gospel, whether here or in the world of spirits, he is
saved" (Ibid., 357). Again the Prophet only promises salvation.
He does not promise celestial glory to spirit prisons' repentant
sinners. Admittedly, in the above quotes, the Prophet is not
talking about those who have been sealed. However, the case still
applies. According to Doctrine and Covenants 76:31, any who
know and partake of God's power and are overcome by the power
of the devil such that they deny the truth and defy God's power
are doomed to suffer forever with the devil and his angels.

Second, the road to celestial glory is paved with good deeds all
the way to the top. To believe that the sealing by the Holy Spirit
of promise means a person can stop serving halfway there is ludi-
crous. The Savior meant what He told His friends, "He that is
greatest among you shall be your servant. And whosoever shall
exalt himself shall be abased; and he that shall humble himself
shall be exalted" (Matt. 23:11–12). Service is what the Gods do.
Sin is at best a prostituted form of self-service which can only buy
one into hell, not heaven. The task of making one's calling and
election sure comes by doing good deeds all the way to the "pearly
gates"—*and beyond.*

No sealing is actually unconditional. One cannot deny the Holy
Ghost or shed innocent blood and be saved from the second
death. However, for those who receive the Holy Spirit of
Promise's sealing "by him who is anointed, unto whom I [God]
have appointed this power and the keys of this priesthood" and
who do not commit the unpardonable sins do receive assurance
that all other sins will be forgiven and they shall be exalted.
However, they shall pay the uttermost farthing for their unrepen-
tant transgressions being "destroyed in the flesh," and "delivered

unto the buffetings of Satan unto the day of redemption" (D&C 132:19, 26). The point is, no one gets a free ride to exaltation. Those who do not serve heaven to the end, will serve in hell until they have learned to serve and serve well.

52. That is, his *exousía*.

Notes to Chapter Seven

1. Ezra Taft Benson, *The Teachings of Ezra Taft Benson* (Salt Lake City: Bookcraft, 1988), 435.

2. C. S. Lewis, *Mere Christianity* (New York: Collier Books, Macmillian Co., 1952), 114.

3. Ibid., 114, italics in the original.

4. Neal A. Maxwell, ". . . *A More Excellent Way*" (Salt Lake City: Deseret Book, 1967), 83.

5. Moffatt, *Love in the New Testament*, 278, and Morris, *Testaments*, 172.

6. Ibid.

7. Harold B. Lee, "Stand Ye in Holy Places," *Ensign*, July 1973, 124.

8. Victor Paul Furnish, *The Love Commandment in the New Testament* (Nashville: Abingdon Press), 43–45.

9. Morris, *Testaments*, 173–74.

10. The Greek word Matthew used is *mammōnas*.

11. Nicoll, ed., *The Expositor's Greek Testament*, 1:124.

12. Maxwell, *Deposition of a Disciple*, 58.

13. The words are *'āhēbh* and *'ahⁱbhāh* respectively.

14. Morris, *Testaments*, 12.

15. H. H. Rowley, *The Faith of Israel* (London: Westminister Publishing, 1956), 65.

16. Morris, *Testaments,* 25.

17. Norman Snaith, *Mercy and Sacrifice* (London: SCM, 1953), 80.

18. The KJV follows the Septuagint, saying, "For the righteous Lord loveth righteousness; his countenance doth behold the upright." The Hebrew shows that he is the one who is beheld through

righteousness.

19. Morris, *Testaments,* 31–32. The first line of the psalm reveals the seat of one's safety. The last line reveals where the heart should be. A person can seek blessing for selfish reasons, but it is love, and love alone, that seeks for the face of God. See also Derek Kidner, *Psalms 1–72* (London: Inter-Varsity Press, 1973), 74.

20. This is the King James translation of the Hebrew *qānāh.*

21. The Joseph Smith Translation translates this as follows: "Thou shalt worship no other god: for the Lord, whose name is Jehovah, is a jealous God." Though it clarifies the name of God, it underscores that He possesses the attribute of "jealousy."

22. Rousas John Rushdoony, *The Institutes of Biblical Law* (n.p.: The Craig Press, 1973), 24.

23. Ibid., 24–25.

24. Richard D. Draper, *Opening the Seven Seals* (Salt Lake City: Deseret Book, 1991), 126.

25. For example, see Revelation 7:1–3, where the destroying angels are held back until the servants of God are sealed against their power, 8:7–13, where the destruction never goes beyond one third; and 9:3–5, where the locusts of Satan cannot hurt the earth nor the righteous and hold power only for a specific period of time.

26. Neal A. Maxwell, *Sermons Not Spoken* (Salt Lake City: Bookcraft, 1985), 70–71.

27. Neal A. Maxwell, *Men and Women of Christ* (Salt Lake City: Bookcraft, 1990), 9.

28. Ibid.

29. Maxwell, *Sermons*, 71.

30. Neal A. Maxwell, *A Wonderful Flood of Light* (Salt Lake City: Bookcraft, 1990), 6.

31. Neal A. Maxwell, *For the Power is in Them* (Salt Lake City: Deseret Book, 1970), 61–62.

32. *Dictionary of the Bible*, ed. J. Hastings; rev. ed. by F. C. Grant and H. H. Rowley (New York: Charles Schribner's Sons, 1963), s.v. "love."

33. The Greek word is *agapē*.
34. Richard Lloyd Anderson, *Guide to Acts and the Apostle's Letters* (Provo, Utah: privately printed, n. d.), n. p.
35. The word is *makrothumeō*.
36. That is, *chrēsteoumai*.
37. The word is *zēloō*.
38. This word is *perpereuomai*.
39. That is what the word *phusioō* means.
40. The word is *aschēmoneō*.
41. The phrase is *ou zētei ta eautēs*.
42. That is, *paroxunō*.
43. The word is *logizomai*.
44. The word is *adikia*.
45. That is a *didaskalos*.
46. That is, a *paidagōgos*.

Notes to Chapter 8

1. Benson, *Teachings,* 357.
2. Draper, *Seven Seals,* 232. The reason cowardice and unfaithfulness bring on the second death is because these people have paid a high price to come to know God and, in the process, have partaken of God's power and known His word. To become unfaithful and cowardly due to the pressure of the world, after God has given them His most precious gifts, brings upon them His most severe judgments. President Joseph F. Smith explored the consequences of turning from God when he asked,

> [B]ut what of those who do believe, repent of their sins, obey the gospel, enter into its covenants, receive the keys of the Priesthood and the knowledge of the truth by revelation and the gift of the Holy Ghost, and afterwards turn away wholly from that light and knowledge? They "become a law unto themselves," and "will to abide in sin;"

of such it is written, "whoso breaketh this covenant, after he hath received it, and altogether turneth therefrom, shall not have forgiveness in this world nor in the world to come." And again, "Thus saith the Lord, concerning all those who know my power, and have been made partakers thereof, and suffered themselves, through the power of the devil, to be overcome, and to deny the truth and defy my power—they are they who are the sons of perdition, of whom I say that it had been better for them never to have been born, for they are vessels of wrath, doomed to suffer the wrath of God, with the devil and his angels in eternity; concerning whom I have said there is no forgiveness in this world nor in the world to come, having denied the Holy Spirit after having received it, and having denied the Only Begotten Son of the Father—having crucified him unto themselves, and put him to an open shame"—D & C. 76:31–35.

Now, there is a difference between this class and those who simply repent not and reject the gospel in the flesh. Of these latter it is written, "they shall be brought forth by the resurrection of the dead, through the triumph and the glory of the Lamb," and "shall be redeemed in the due time of the Lord after the sufferings of his wrath." But of the others it is said, "they shall not be redeemed," for "they are the only ones on whom the second death shall have any power." The others, never having been redeemed from the first, cannot be doomed to the second death, or in other words cannot be made to suffer eternally the wrath of God, without hope of redemption through repentance, but must continue to suffer the first death until they repent, and are redeemed therefrom through the power of the Atonement and the gospel of salvation, thereby being brought to the possession of all the keys and blessings to which they will be capable of attaining or to which they may be entitled, through the mercy, justice and power of the everlasting God; or, on the other hand, forever remain bound in the chains of spiritual darkness, bondage and banishment from his presence, kingdom and glory. The "temporal death" is one thing, and the "spiritual death" is another thing. The body may be dissolved and become extinct as an organism, although the elements of which it is composed are indestructible or eternal, but I hold it as self-evident that the spiritual organism is an eternal, immortal being, destined to enjoy eternal happiness and a fulness of joy, or suffer the wrath of God, and misery—a just condemnation, eternally. Adam became spiritually dead, yet he lived to endure it until freed therefrom by the power of the atonement, through repentance, etc. Those upon whom the second death shall fall will live to suffer and endure it, but without hope of redemption (Smith, *Gospel Doctrine,* 15–16).

3. Hugh Nibley, *Collected Works of Hugh Nibley,* vol. 3: *The World and the Prophets* (Salt Lake City: Deseret Book, 1987), 264.

4. Edwin Markham, "Outwitted," cited in *Teachings of Gordon B. Hinckley* (Salt Lake City: Deseret Book, 1997), 317.

5. Arthur Henry King, *The Abundance of the Heart* (Salt Lake City: Bookcraft, 1986), 255.

6. Maxwell, *Give Thee Experience,* 14–15.

INDEX

Accuser, Satan is the, 15-16, 145, n. 26
Adam and Eve, length of time spent in garden, 144, n. 12
Affection, 64-65
Agency, 35
Alma the Elder, 104
Alma the Younger, 164, n. 10
Anderson, Richard Lloyd, 175, n. 34
Andrus, Hyrum L., 165, n. 15
Apostates, 171, n. 49
Aristotle, 67
Atonement: full cost of, and Savior's power to back away, 40-44; need for, 47-48; was eternal yet personal, 51; is manifestation of God's love, 55-56, agony of the, 151-52, n. 1; 153, n. 11. *See also* Redemption
Authority, 154, n. 3; 154-55, n. 4; 155, n. 5; and power, 56-58, 59-60

Baptism, 22-23
Beatitudes, 147, n. 1; as steps to happiness, 21-22, 33
Benson, Ezra Taft, 17-18, 147, n. 31; on pride, 111; on gospel principles leading to joy, 134
Blessedness, 147-48, nn. 1, 2; steps to, 21-33

Boredom, 13
Born again, 48, 94
Bornkamm, Gunther, 157, n. 1

Cain, 17; rules over Satan, 146-47, n. 30
Calling and election, 163, n. 4; meaning of, 82-83; steps necessary to make, sure, 84-95; and the more sure word of prophecy, 95-100; interrelationship of, with love and joy, 106-107. *See also* Holy Spirit of Promise; More sure word of prophecy; Sealing
Callousness, 123-24
Charity, 68-69, 80, 100; Christ's, 69-71; required to partake of divine nature, 94-95; need for, 124-25; fulfills the whole law, 126-29. *See also* Love
Chesterton, G. K., 113
Chosen, 83, 163-64, n. 7
Cicero, 67
Comforter, 16, 23-24. *See also* Holy Ghost; Second Comforter
Commandment, to love, 109-11
Commandments: obedience to, 36, 50; God's, symbolized by rod of iron, 134

Courage, in face of persecution, 32-33
Cowardice, 32; 176, n. 2
Cross, taking up one's, 151, n. 17

Darkness, spiritual, 92-93
Day of Pentecost, 87
Death, 5-6; is result of sin, 44-46; second, 176-78, n. 2
Deception, of Satan, 17-18
Delight, contrasted to joy, 7-8
Desire, precedes deed, 29
Destruction, God sets limits on, 137; 175, n. 25
Diligence, 89
Dishonesty, story of convert who overcame, 78-80
Divine nature, steps for partaking of the, 89-95
Draper, Richard D., 165, nn. 16, 18; 175, n. 24; on the second death, 176, n. 2

Earnest, 105; 172, n. 50
Earth, 131
Eden, was a joyless place, 9
Enos, 103-104
Envy, 76
Eternal life, assurance of, 26. *See also* Calling and election; Exaltation

Eusebius, 156, n. 12
Exaltation, 18. *See also* Eternal life
Expiation, 55-56; 154, nn. 1, 2

Faith: of woman with issue of blood, 58-60; of woman who overcame dishonesty, 79; equired to partake of divine nature, 89; need for, 124-25; relationship of love to, 130
Faithfulness, amidst persecution, 32-33
Fall of Adam, purpose of, 5-6, 9-10, 35
Fear: is antonym of love, 124-25; has nothing to do with God's power to bind, 131; overcoming, of joy, 136-38
Fellowship, 152, n. 5; steps to full, with Christ, 37-40
Fire, cloven tongues of, 86, 87
Foreknowledge, God's, 83-84
Foreordination, 82; 164, n. 10
Forgiveness, 27-28; and the unpardonable sin, 170-72, n. 49
Freedom, of choice, 35
Friendship, 67-68; 160, n. 22
Fulness of joy: is through gospel plan, 18-19; love brings us to, 63; love and eternal life are prerequisites to, 77. *See also* Joy

Furnish, Victor Paul, 174, n. 8

Gifts of the Spirit, 117-18
Glory, of God, 85-87
God: and source of His joy, 11, 13; and His feelings regarding loss of children, 13; is a jealous God, 121-23
Godliness, required to partake of divine nature, 91-92; power of, 98
Golden rule, 31
Grace, 27-28; 85; 153-54, n. 16; acceptance of, by obeying commandments, 50-52; need for, 74-75; false ideas regarding, 102-103; of God upon Son, 150, n. 10
Great and spacious building, 102-103; symbolizes pride of world, 134-36

Happiness: difference between, and joy, 6-8, 10-11; is the appeal of heaven, 12; Beatitudes as steps to, 21-22, 33. *See also* Joy
Heart, symbolizes desires, 29
Heaven, appeal of, 11-12, 13
Holiness, 91-92, 166, n. 31
Holy Ghost: gift of, 22-23; is the First Comforter, 23-24; Father expresses grace

by giving, 28; purifies, 29-30; and day of Pentecost, 87; denial of the, 171, n. 49. *See also* Comforter
Holy Spirit of Promise, 25-26, 88; sealing by the, 99-100; 101; 105-106; 168, n. 41; 168-69, n. 42; 172-73, n. 51. *See also* Second Comforter
Hope, need for, 124-25
Humility, 111-14

Iniquity, makes love wax cold, 123-24
Intelligence, God's, 86

Jealousy, a God of, 121-23
Jesus Christ: was greatest example of mercy, 27; grew from grace to grace, 28; steps to full fellowship with, 37-40; power of, to heal, 58-60; cost of love to, 61. *See also* Atonement; Redemption.
Job, 6-7, 15-16
Joint-heirs with Christ, 38-40
Joy: is the purpose and meaning of life, 2, 6, 139-40; difference between happiness and, 6-8, 10-11; contrasted with pleasure, 7-8, 143, n. 8; can grow through trials, 9-11; and service, 11-14, 138; finding, in the

Church, 76; inter-relationship of love, calling and election, and, 106-107; overcoming fear of, 136-38; source of God's, 139. *See also* Fulness of joy; Happiness

Justice, cannot be robbed by mercy, 119; God's jealousy is guarantee of, 122

Justification, 51-52, 84

Kindness, brotherly, required to partake of divine nature, 92-94

King, Arthur Henry, 138

Kittel, Gerhard, 154, n. 2; 155, n. 6

Knowledge: of God, 84-88; 89; 95; 98; 165, nn. 12, 13; required to partake of divine nature, 90

Kolob, time of, 144, n. 12

Korihor, 17

Lamb's book of life, 101;170, nn. 46, 47

Lane, William L., 156, n. 12

Last days, opposition of, 32

Law of Moses, 129-30

Law: only one, 44-45; consequences of breaking, 51; God's, and His jealousy, 122-23; love fulfills the, and the prophets, 125-30

Leaders, following Lord's, 22

Lee, Harold B., 22, 99, 114

Lehi's vision: the tree in, 53-55, 63, 77, 81, 100-102, 109; the great and spacious building in, 102-103; and the fruit of love, 103-104; and obstacles to reaching the tree, 133-36

Lewis, C. S., 158, nn. 4, 9; on affection, 65; on friendship, 67; on humility, 112; on Satan's desires, 145-47, n. 30

Light, 86-87, 92-93

Lindbergh, Anne Morrow, 118

Love: meaning of life is joy and, 2, 139-40; Atonement grew out of, 43-44, 55-56; Lehi's tree symbolized, 54-55, 77; cost of Lord's, 61; brings us to fulness of joy, 63; scriptural understanding of, 64-71; parables illustrating, 71-77; Savior's, 84; connection between light and, 86-87; perfect, 100, 101-102; 170, n. 47; inter-relationship of, calling and election, and joy, 106-107; commandment to, 109-11; of self, 111, 112-13; of neighbor, 114-17; is directly associated with God's gifts, 117-18; tough, 118-21; God's, as unconditional vs.

conditional, 119, 121; waxes cold with iniquity, 123-24; fulfills the law and the prophets, 125-30; as sole power of the universe, 130-32; Greek words expressing a dimension of, 157-58, n. 3; 158, nn. 4, 5, 6, 7, 10, 11; 159, nn. 12, 14; 160 nn. 21, 28, 29; 160-61; n. 30; 161 nn. 31, 32, 34, 35; 162, n. 37; is context of commandment to be perfect, 162, n. 42. *See also* Charity

Lying, story of convert who overcame, 78-80

Mammon, 116-17

Markham, Edwin, poem by, 137

Marriage, celestial, 39-40. *See also* Exaltation

Martyrdom, 94; Peter knew of impending, 163, n. 2

Maxwell, Neal A., 145, n. 21;147, n. 32; 175, nn. 26, 27, 28, 29, 30; on joy, 11, 14; on the full weight of the Atonement, 42; on love, 113; on using wisdom in our service, 118; on faith, hope, and charity, 125; on source of God's joy, 139

McConkie, Bruce R., 149, n. 6; 163, nn. 5, 6;

164, nn. 8, 9; on being joint-heirs with Christ, 38-39; on celestial marriage, 39-40

McKay, David O.: on showing love for God through service, 114; on joy vs. pleasure, 143, n. 8

Meaning of life, is love and joy, 2, 139-40

Meek, 24, 27

Merciful, are blessed, 26-28

Mercy, 27-28; 149, n. 8; will not rob justice, 119

Misery, Satan desires, of all, 14-17

Mists of darkness, symbolize temptations, 133

Moffatt, James, 159, n. 15; 174, n. 5

More sure word of prophecy, 95-97; relationship between calling and election and, 97-100. *See also* Calling and election; Holy Spirit of Promise

Moroni, 104

Morris, Leon, 119; 157, n. 2; 159, nn. 13, 18; 160, nn. 19, 20, 27; 161, n. 34; 162, nn. 36, 40; 163, nn. 46, 47, 48; 174, nn. 5, 6, 9, 16, 19

Mortality, 5-6

Moses, 85-86

Mourning, 149, n. 4; as sorrow for sin, 23-24

Nephi, son of Helaman, 25

Nephi, son of Lehi, 53-54

Nephite disciples, 104

Nibley, Charles W., 168, n. 39

Nibley, Hugh: on fear of joy, 136; on coming out of the world; 167, n. 32

Nygren, Anders, 162, n. 38

Obedience, love and, are twins, 125

Opposition: necessity for, 9-11; and the great and spacious building, 102-103

Otten, L. G. and C. M. Caldwell, 167, n. 32

Pain, is what Satan seeks to inflict, 16-17

Parable: of the five hundred pennies, 46-53; of the prodigal son, 71-72; of the workers in the vineyard, 73; rabbis', of the skillful worker, 73-74; of the publican and the Pharisee, 75; modern, of two brothers, 75-76; of the good Samaritan, 114

Paraklete, 149, n. 5

Patience, 166, n. 28; required to partake of divine nature, 91

Paul, 104; 164, n. 10

Peace, 165, n. 15

Peacemakers, 30-31

Perfection: process of nearing, 18-19; and love, 71; 162, n. 42

Persecution, 31-33

Perseverance, 91

Peter, 81; knew he would die a martyr, 163, n. 2

Plan of salvation, 83-84

Plato, 159, n. 16

Pleasure, contrasted with joy, 7-8; 143, n. 8; of a pyromaniac, 13-14

Poor in spirit: story of woman who was, 21, 33; are blessed, 23

Power, 154, n. 3; 154-55, n. 4; access to godly, 25; of Savior to back away from Atonement, 40-44; to become God's children, 56-58; Lord's healing, 59; interplay of faith, authority, and, 60; of Lord to heal, 79; love as the sole, of the universe, 130-32

Premortality, and foreordination, 82

Pride, 111-12; 148, n. 3; of the world symbolized by great and spacious building, 133, 134-36

Priesthood, 98

Prodigal son, parable of the, 71-72

Progression, beyond the grave, 166, n. 28

Propitiation, 55-56

Punishment: and God's love, 119-20; sin brings its own, 120

Pure in heart, 28-30

Purification, through the Holy Ghost, 29-30

Purity, 150-51, n. 11
Purpose of life, according
     to Lehi, 5-6
Pyromaniac, 13-14

Rebirth. *See* Born again
Redemption: need for,
     35-36, 47-48; leads
     to full fellowship with
     Christ, 37-40. *See
     also* Atonement
Relationship, with Savior
     or Father, 114
Resurrection, Joseph
     Smith's vision of the,
     89
Righteousness, brings joy,
     14; hungering and
     thirsting after, 24-26
Roberts, B. H.: on neces-
     sity of opposition, 9-
     10; on joy, 11
Robinson, Stephen E.,
     153, n. 16;165, n. 15
Rod of iron, 134
Romance, 65-66, 68-69
Romney, Marion G., 89;
     165, n. 15; 167, n.
     38
Rougemont, Denis de,
     160, n. 22
Rowley, H. H., 174, n. 15
Rushdoony, Rousas John,
     175, nn. 22, 23

Sacramental blessing, 29
Sacrifice, and service, 140-
     41
Sade, Marquis de, 16-17
Sadism, 16-17
Salvation, fulness of joy
     requires, 18-19
Sanctification, 151, n. 14
Satan: casting out of, 12-
     13, 15; desires misery

of all, 14-17; is the
     accuser, 15-16;
     deceptions of, 17-18;
     desires of; 145-47, n.
     30; Cain rules over;
     146-47, n. 30
Screwtape, 145, n. 30
Sealing: by the Holy
     Spirit of Promise, 99;
     100; 101-102; 105-
     106; 168, n. 41; 168-
     69, n. 42; no, is
     unconditional, 172-
     73, n. 51
Second Comforter, 25-26,
     30, 38, 88. *See also*
     Holy Spirit of
     Promise
Self-control: of the meek,
     24, 27; and temper-
     ance, 90-91
Selfishness, 123, 138
Service: joy and, 11-14,
     138; and love of
     neighbor, 114, 116,
     125; is directly associ-
     ated with God's gifts,
     117-18; stories of
     unselfish, 137-38,
     140-41; helps us
     overcome fear of joy,
     137-38; and sacri-
     fice, 140-41
Sin: cost of, 44-46; brings
     its own punishment,
     120; the unpardon-
     able, 170-72, n. 49;
     wilful, after receiving
     knowledge, 172-73,
     n. 51
Slavery, 37-38; 152, nn. 2,
     3
Smith, Joseph, 84; 164, n.
     11; on happiness, 6,
     14; on fruition of joy,

7; on approaching
     perfection, 18-19;
     Lord sealed upon, his
     exaltation, 26, 104;
     on steps toward exal-
     tation, 30; on the
     Second Comforter,
     30; on Savior as the
     Creator, 38; regarding
     hope of the ancient
     Saints, 60; on Peter,
     81; on knowledge,
     85; and vision of the
     resurrection, 89; on
     calling and election,
     98-99; on need for
     perfect love, 101; on
     false ideas regarding
     grace, 102-103; on
     progression beyond
     the grave, 166, n. 28;
     thoughts of, on
     Lamb's book of life,
     170, nn. 46, 47; on
     the unpardonable sin,
     170-71, n. 49; on
     limits on which the
     Spirit can seal, 172,
     n. 51
Smith, Joseph F., on the
     second death, 176-
     78, n. 2
Smith, Joseph Fielding,
     168, n. 41; on the
     Holy Spirit of
     Promise, 99; on Satan
     being subject to Cain,
     147, n. 30; thoughts
     of, on Lamb's book of
     life, 170, n. 46
Snaith, Norman, 174, n. 17
Sons of perdition, 176-77,
     n. 2
Story: of seminary
     student's talk on

trials, 8-9; of woman who was poor in spirit, 21, 33; of woman with issue of blood, 58-60; of divorced mother with lying problem, 78-80; of two boys helping a neighbor woman, 137-38; of student feeling that service was no sacrifice, 140-41; of man's joy in recognition received by wife, 141-42. *See also* Parable

Talmage, James E., 156, n. 13
Taylor, John, on the more sure word of prophecy, 96
Temperance, required to partake of divine nature, 90-91
Temptations, are a major impediment to achieving joy, 133-34
Ten Commandments, 129
Testimony, 85, 88, 90
Time, as reckoned by God, 144, n. 12
Top, Brent, 87
Torrey, Charles Cutler, 162, n. 42
Trials, 144, n. 15; righteousness doesn't prevent, 8; joy can grow through, 9-11
Truth, 86

Unfaithfulness, 32, 152, 176, n. 2
Unhappiness: joy possible during period of, 10-

11; things contributing to, 12

Virtue: God's, 87; required to partake of divine nature, 89-90

War in heaven, 12-13, 15
Wealth, 24, 116
Well-being, 6, 7
Wickedness, can't lead to happiness, 7
Willingness, 29
World, coming out of the, 167, n. 32

Young, Brigham, 14; on God's testing us, 41; on more sure word of prophecy, 97; thoughts of, on Lamb's book of life, 170, n. 46

Zabim, 155, n.10